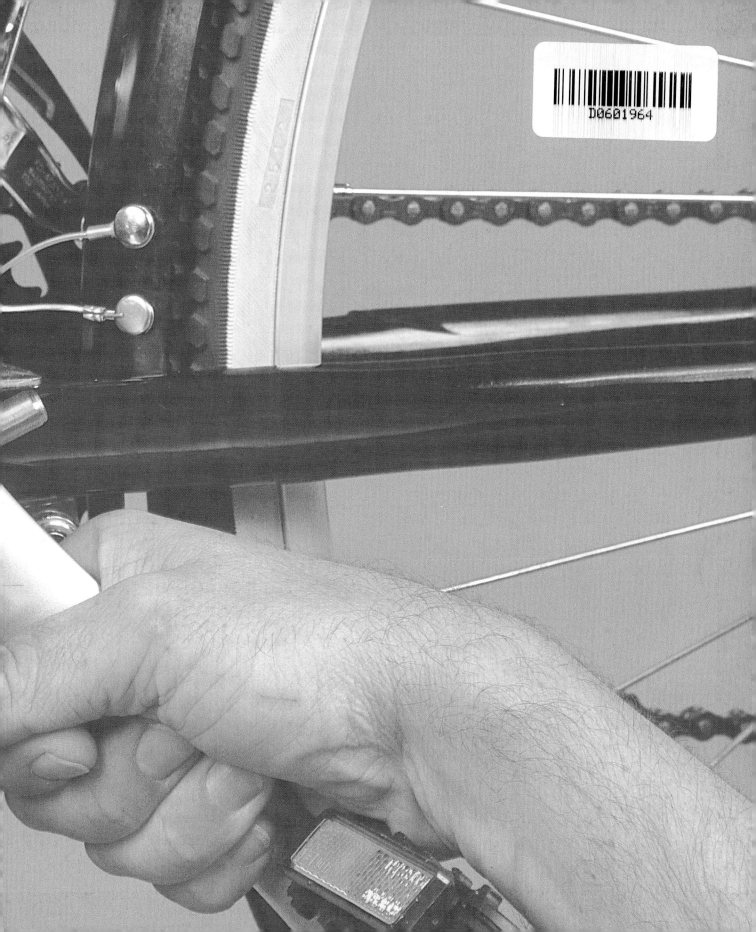

THE
BICYCLE
BOOK

The complete maintenance guide

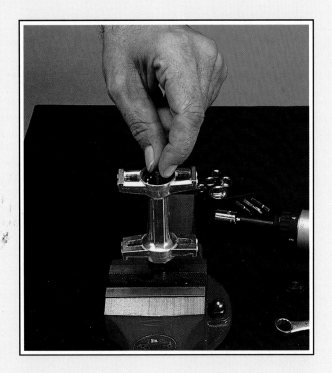

THE
BICYCLE
BOOK

The complete
maintenance guide

Geoff Apps

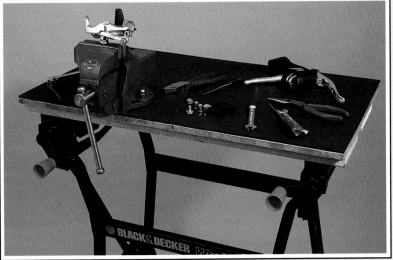

CRESCENT BOOKS
New York • Avenel, New Jersey

CREDITS

This 1993 edition published by Crescent Books, Distributed by the Outlet Book Company, Inc., A Random House Company, 40 Engelhard Avenue, Avenel, New Jersey 07001

Random House New York•Toronto•London•Sydney•Auckland.

ISBN O 517 08743 X

All correspondence concerning the content of this volume should be addressed to:
Salamander Books Ltd.,
129-137 York Way, London N7 9LG.

Editor: Will Steeds
US Technical consultant: Frank Berto
Designers: Paul Johnson, John Heritage, Geoff Apps
Photographers: Sue Darlow, Barbara Berkowitz, Jason Smith
Illustrations: Geoff Apps
Index: Edward Leeson
Typesetting: Calligrafix, Scotland
Color separation: Scantrans Pte. Ltd., Singapore

Printed and bound in Singapore

Author: Geoff Apps

Geoff Apps has always been fascinated with how things work and this, coupled with a life-long delight in bicycling, has led him to become well-versed in bicycle technology. Apps is regarded by many bicyclists as the British pioneer of off-road bicycling, having designed and built a precursor to the mountain bike.

Apps' writing career began when he edited and published the cross-country bicycling fan magazine, *Making Tracks*. After that, he worked for *New Cyclist* magazine, eventually becoming Technical Editor.

Apps lives in a cottage by the River Tweed in Scotland where he runs courses on bicycle maintenance, and enjoys bicycling the traffic-free lanes.

Technical consultant: Frank Berto

Frank Berto is recognized throughout the U.S. as a leading expert on bicycle technology. He has written extensively for the top selling *Bicycling* magazine and has acted as its Engineering Editor. He is currently Engineering Editor of *Bicycle USA*, the magazine of the American League of Wheelmen. Berto is the author of *Bicycling Magazine's Complete Guide to Upgrading Your Bike*.

CONTENTS

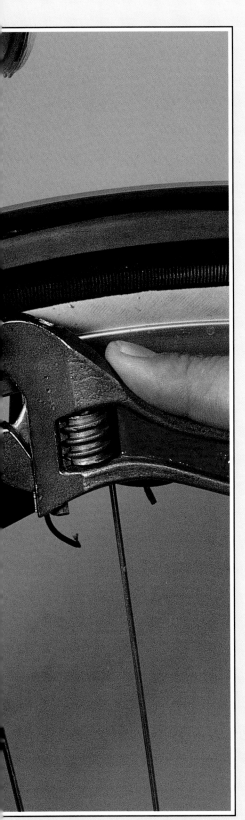

Workshop safety

- Ensure that all equipment is well-maintained
- Store all tools and equipment safely away when not in use
- Do not use any electrical equipment that has a damaged cord or a broken or loose plug
- Ensure that all electrical equipment is properly grounded
- Ensure that any equipment with a 2-wire cord is double-insulated
- If extension cords are used, ensure that the connecting plugs are secure and that the cord is correctly rated for the job
- If you use an extension cord on a self-rewinding drum, ensure that it is UL-rated
- Never use any electric equipment in damp or wet conditions
- Wear safety glasses when sawing, drilling or grinding hard materials
- Wear safety glasses when pouring or using paint, degreaser, rust inhibitor and other such fluids
- Wear safety gloves when working with degreaser, rust inhibitor and other such fluids
- Use glue and adhesives and other such potentially hazardous substances with special care - they may give off flammable vapors. Use only in well-ventilated spaces
- Always follow the manufacturer's instructions when working with tools, equipment and chemicals
- Ensure that your workshop, or workshop area, is equipped with a fire extinguisher
- Keep children away from the workshop area

INTRODUCTION

A well-maintained bicycle is a pleasure to ride and rarely needs to be repaired. By spending a little time looking after your bicycle, you will not only be able to enjoy your bicycling to the full – you will also save a considerable amount of time and money.

Many bicyclists carry out maintenance tasks on their bicycles on a random basis – that is, when they have the time, and when it occurs to them that something needs to be adjusted or looked at. It is much more effective, however, to establish a program of check, service and overhaul routines that will ensure that every part and mechanism of your bicycle receives attention on a regular basis. Once you get into the habit of doing this, you will soon find that maintaining your bicycle takes very little time – and, perhaps as important – that you enjoy working on your bicycle as much as you enjoy riding it!

I have planned the book so the maintenance requirements for different areas of the bicycle are dealt with in easy reference, self-contained sections. Each section starts with a brief description of the function of the particular component, then continues with specific advice on what needs checking on a weekly basis, on what needs to be serviced every four to six weeks, and on what you should thoroughly overhaul every six months or so. The Weekly check, Regular service, and Overhaul routine checklists that are included at the beginning of the maintenance section summarize what needs to be done, and when; they will help you to ensure that what needs to be done, gets done. The first section of the book, meanwhile, provides advice on setting up a workshop in your house. Again, some careful planning will save much wasted time (and money) later on – and will result in your having a workshop that is convenient to use, but which enables you to avoid getting in the way of other people living in the house.

The maintenance section features very many step-by-step photographs, which show exactly how to carry out particular tasks. For the majority of these photographs, I have used a well-equipped sports bicycle (of a type which is suitable for commuting, leisurely trail riding, and even long-distance touring). Because there are so many different types of bicycle available today, it is quite likely that your bicycle will differ from this example in several respects. The important thing is to look for the similarities so that you develop an understanding of the mechanical principles that apply to all types of bicycle.

It is also necessary to note that metric sizes have become standard for some bicycle parts which are manufactured and/or sold in the U.S. The majority of parts, however, continue to be measured in English sizes. Where appropriate, both metric and English sizes have been listed.

Throughout the book, I use certain terms which have very particular definitions. It is important to make clear what I mean when I use them, as follows:

- **Check.** Check to see that the part or assembly is functioning correctly.
- **Service.** Adjustments (including lubrication) which are required to make a part or assembly function correctly, but which do not involve dismantling the item.
- **Overhaul.** To dismantle, clean, regrease, lube, reassemble and make final adjustments to a part or assembly.
- **Refit.** Refit the original part on the bicycle.
- **Renew or replace.** To fit a new part or assembly in place of the original.
- **Right-/left-hand side**. All such directions assume that the reader is standing at the rear of the bicycle, looking forward.

Finally, remember that your bicycle provides not only a cheap, fast and reliable means of transportation, but sport and recreation as well. Knowing that the bicycle you ride is efficient, serviceable and safe – and that you alone are responsible for this – will become a source of great satisfaction. Have fun!

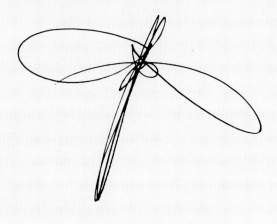

GEOFF APPS

It is often wise to go through a check routine before embarking on a tour of any length and, along with all the other travel arrangements, you may find yourself having to do this late in the day. Moreover, you may discover that you have to make a repair and that the job takes longer than expected. It is at such times that you will most appreciate having a well-equipped and well-stocked workshop. But what will be most appreciated is that it is arranged for maximum convenience and access.

Suitable areas
The first thing you need for maintenance is space – and more than you would at first imagine. Your workshop area should ideally be located indoors, to provide a minimum of comfort and to allow you to work on your bicycles at any time, day or night, whatever the weather. The space used must allow you easy access to your bicycle; several tasks need you to work on one side of the bicycle, then the other, and back again. So it is important that you can get round at one end or the other and, ideally, at both. So choose an area that will provide you with sufficient space to allow you to move around like this.

The ideal place for setting up your workshop is in a utility room or garage. If these are large enough, you can set aside an area within them as a permanent workshop. Few cyclists enjoy the luxury of having an indoor area that can be used solely for bicycle maintenance, however, so you should consider buying workshop equipment that is easily dismantled for storage or transportation, which can be set up in some other room in your house.

If you have to use a room that is shared with other people, you will need to protect any tables, work surfaces or shelves that you use. Over the years I have used a number of materials for this purpose, such as plastic sheeting, cardboard, newspaper, and so on. The best material

I have found, though, is rubber matting which is about ⅟₁₆in. thick. This has clear advantages over the other available materials: the matting lies flat, remains stable and provides an impact-absorbing non-slip surface. The floor of the area you use, especially if it is carpeted, can be covered with a large piece of rubber matting. And if you use the same room and work surfaces regularly, it can be cut to specific sizes with a sharp knife or scissors. After work, it should be cleaned as soon as possible with soapy water, because oil-based lubricants will tend to destroy the rubber quite quickly. However, if you are in a hurry, this task can safely be deferred for a day or two. For storage the matting can be rolled up with a couple of straps tied around it, and a carrying strap can be run between these for transportation. It is quite expensive to buy new rubber matting, but it is often available second-hand at a reasonable price from large printing factories, where it is often used on printing machines.

Of course, when the weather is fine, there are few better ways of enjoying bicycle maintenance than working out of doors. The transportable nature of the workshop I describe here makes this quite feasible. Again, rubber matting to cover your working area will help prevent the loss of small parts, or damage to the lawn.

Facilities needed
After the space requirements, the need for good light must be taken into account. Ideally, your workshop should have a good source of natural light. However, there will also be a need for area electric light-sources as well.

These area lights should be sup-

▶ Rubber matting lies flat because it is quite heavy. However, it can be rolled up and tied with a couple of straps and, with a carrying strap run between them, the roll can be carried over the shoulder to be stored or transported as you wish.

plemented by a couple of adjustable spotlights, which will be used to throw light onto the specific area of work. I have found that two 100W lamps are more than adequate. Clip-on spotlights will prove useful; these can be clipped to part of the bicycle and focused onto the area on which you are working.

Head-mounted flashlights are still relatively unfamiliar in the home setting, but they are surprisingly useful for a number of bicycle maintenance jobs: many operations are made easier if pinpoint lighting is directed exactly onto the place you require. The output of the more common 4.5-volt flashlights can be boosted by replacing the standard bulb with a halogen bulb. Alternatively, for really clear light, you can invest in a 12-volt rechargeable system designed for night riding, and use it for the latter as well as maintenance.

An electric power source is essential for any workshop, although it need not be close to your work area if you add an extension cord with three or four outlets to your workshop kit.

Degreasing and cleaning of small assemblies and parts is best done using a water-soluble degreasing fluid, which requires quantities of

▼ The length of a regular adult's bicycle will be just under 6ft 6in. To have clear access to both sides of the bicycle you should be able to move around it at each end as well. A minimum of 1ft 8in. (but preferably more) should be allowed for this, which means that the overall length required for your working area will be not far short of 10ft.

Most of the maintenance tasks require easy access to both sides of the bicycle; you will need about 3ft 3in. of space on either side of your workstand. So, multiplying the width required by the length, a minimum area of about 64 sq. ft is needed, simply to have effective access to your bicycle when it is mounted in the workstand.

Make a further allowance for a workbench, tool storage and also for space to maneuver the bicycle, whether complete, or partly dismantled. An area of no less than 22 sq. ft should be sufficient. By combining the bench and workstand, and wall-mounting the tool storage cupboard, this space requirement can be reduced to some extent.

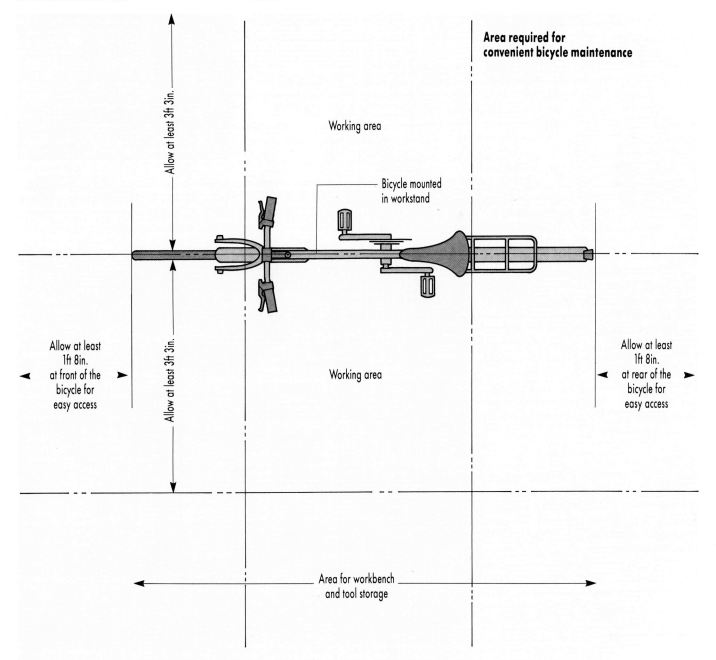

Area required for convenient bicycle maintenance

Allow at least 3ft 3in.

Working area

Bicycle mounted in workstand

Allow at least 3ft 3in.

Allow at least 1ft 8in. at front of the bicycle for easy access

Working area

Allow at least 1ft 8in. at rear of the bicycle for easy access

Area for workbench and tool storage

rinsing water. The kitchen sink is ideal for this purpose (but make sure you clean it afterwards). However, if you cannot use the sink, a collection of metal pans and basins will be needed. For easy storage, these should stack together, and ideally they should be made of stainless steel.

The workbench

The cornerstone of a bicycle workshop is the workbench, which must provide a firm and stable work surface. If you are lucky enough to be able to set up a workshop in a designated room of sufficient area, you should really consider a fixed workbench that is made to measure. You can either make your own, or employ a cabinet maker to install one for you. The secret of a good workbench is that it be very stable. Stability can be achieved by using vast quantities of sturdy wood, but if the bench can be anchored to a solid wall, then a less substantial construction will prove quite adequate.

Most people will have to do their bicycle maintenance in a family house, so it is unlikely there will be a space you can devote exclusively to your hobby. I therefore base my workshop recommendations around this likelihood. In the case of a workbench, the best solution is to purchase a folding model, such as the Black & Decker Workmate.

Stand options

It is vital that you have a means of holding your bicycle upright and steady and with the rear wheel, at least, raised off the ground. The latter is important because it will enable you to operate and adjust the gears while the bicycle is stationary – the cranks will be free to rotate, and the gear control cables and shifters will operate unobstructed.

Bicycle stands

A number of bicycle stands are available which simply hold the bicycle steady with the rear wheel raised. It is possible to make your own from wood, but if you choose to purchase one, there are three styles available.

The first type has a pair of splayed legs, and it fits under the bottom bracket with a forward extending arm which hooks over the down-tube. The stand relies on the weight of the bicycle to give stability. A second type consists of a vertical arm with two hooks, one at a height for the chain-stay and another higher up for the seatstay; the base is formed by two splayed arms, which lie flat on the ground under the rear wheel.

The third type uses two 'cups' on the ends of a pair of wire supports; a cup fits over each end of the rear

▲ Head-mounted flashlights are gaining in popularity for night riding. In the workshop, many operations are made easier using this source of lighting, which you can direct exactly where you require.

▼ If you do not have the space available to install a permanent workbench, your best option is to buy a Black & Decker Workmate. The Workmate folds away easily when not in use.

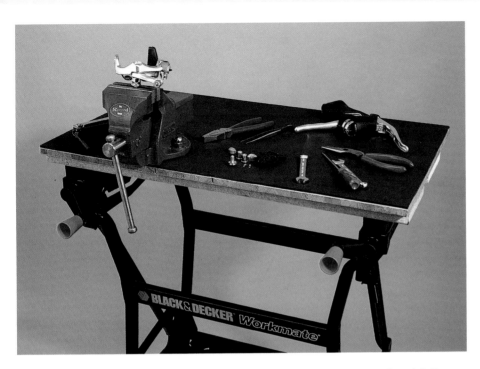

▲ It is possible to mount a bench vise onto a folding workbench by making a simple top adapter. The adapter is placed on top and held firmly by the clamping action. This is also the perfect site for mounting a drill stand.

▼ A bicycle stand such as this will simply hold your bicycle upright with the rear wheel off the ground. This type is useful for when you are working on more than one bicycle or if you need somewhere to stand it while you use the workbench for other jobs.

wheel axle. This latter design, unlike the others, does not allow the rear wheel to be removed. None of these stands allow the front wheel to be removed.

If your workshop has a solid wall, consider installing a wall-mounted bicycle holder. These are designed for storage of diamond-framed bicycles, but can be useful for maintenance as well (although they only allow access to one side of your bicycle at a time, of course). A wall-mounted holder requires strong mountings, so be sure that the wall, and the fittings you use, are well up to the job.

You can also make your own wall-mounted holder by fixing two metal shelf brackets to the wall and mounting a shelf onto them. Fix two battens to the shelf at right-angles to the wall, with V cuts at the forward end, far enough from the wall for your bicycle to rest in.

If space is at a premium, you can buy a demountable wall holder. However, with this type, the receiving bracket remains in place on the wall when the holder is removed, which may be considered unsightly.

Bicycle workstands
A bicycle workstand will raise your bicycle to a comfortable height and hold it steady, so it can be worked on easily while you are in a standing position. The majority of types will permit the bicycle to be rotated when it is mounted in the workstand, allowing access to areas that would normally be awkward to work on.

There are quite a few models of free-standing bicycle workstand available from a wide variety of makers. Many are of a simple tubular design, and they are easily dismantled for storage and transportation – which makes them ideal for the amateur bicycle mechanic. If you want to take your bicycle maintenance more seriously, and you have a permanent workshop space, you may consider buying one of the professional workstands on the market, of which there are several. These are usually substantial constructions providing a rock-solid mounting for your bicycle, but they are only suitable if you have a concrete floor into which you can fix the stand. This type of stand is expensive and so they are usually only found in professional bicycle workshops.

If you are considering using a folding workbench because economy of space is paramount, one very well-designed type fits into the Black & Decker Workmate, making an ideal and economical workstand option. As with many good workstands, the Kestrel Workmate provides a firm mounting for your bicycle, and means that the space required for a separate workstand can be saved. The top of the folding workbench is available for the tools and components you are working with. There is also an optional free-standing base made of metal for the Workmate-type stand, which can be purchased as funds allow. The drawback with this design of workstand – where the bottom bracket rests in a holder with the down tube clamped to a forward extending arm – is that the bicycle cannot be rotated. However, to my mind, the space-saving convenience of the design outweighs this.

▲ Where space is limited, or you need a pack-away workshop for easy transportation, the type that fits straight into a Black & Decker Workmate makes an economical purchase.

▼ Many free-standing workstands allow the bicycle to be rotated so that you can work on normally inaccessible areas. These are ideal if you plan to progress to more advanced maintenance.

General tools

There are several general tools which you will need to use very frequently and which you should therefore have in your workshop. Some of these are available from bicycle shops, but the majority can be bought at a local DIY store. Because you will be making heavy use of them, these tools should be of as high a quality as you can afford. Do not disregard second-hand tools, though; provided they have been looked after as yours will be, and are in good condition, they will probably give you long service. Second-hand tools will, of course, be very much cheaper than new tools. Look out for them at garage sales and in the flea markets.

Special tools

There are also some special tools, which, because they make specific tasks so much easier, are well worth purchasing. Such special tools are often quite expensive so, where appropriate, I mention when general tools can be substituted for them. (Bear in mind that to do the latter will always involve a compromise; it may not be as easy to carry out the task using a general tool, and there is also a greater risk of damaging the components if great care is not taken.) In the maintenance section of this book the special tools shown are examples of the type available.

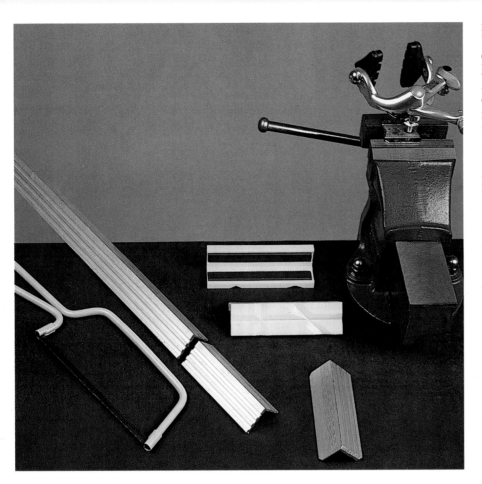

▲ A steel-jawed vise can damage aluminum components or steel threads, so always use a pair of plastic or aluminum vise clamps. They are easy to make yourself from pieces of aluminum angle.

You will find tools for sale with the same name and function, but which may look rather different.

Bench vise

A bench vise is, as its name suggests, mounted on the workbench and, as the maintenance section shows, it is a valuable tool. Its purpose is to hold components steady while you are working on them. Buy good quality, although economies can be made with regard to size. A quality bench vise is usually made from cast iron and fitted with removable knurled steel jaws. If you are using a fold-away workbench, it is wise to avoid buy-ing a bench vise that is too heavy. However, do buy one of a reasonable size: the size of the jaws is indicative of its ability to hold items firmly, and one with 3in. jaws is about the right size for bicycle components.

Cast aluminum bench vises used to be available, but can now only be bought second-hand. They offer rea-sonable size, yet remain relatively light in weight. A cast aluminum bench vise is quite suitable for the type of bicycle maintenance work you will be doing.

If you buy a steel-jawed vise, it is most important that you fit it with a pair of plastic or aluminum vise clamps. These sometimes feature a magnetic strip to keep them in posi-tion. Vise clamps are very easily and economically made by cutting down a length of aluminum angle. It is more than likely that vise clamps will become damaged quite quickly, so cut several sets at once from the length you buy. Because they are made from a softer material, vise clamps will protect small, delicate items from damage when you tighten the vise on them.

There are two ways to mount a bench vise onto your workbench. Most mechanics' vises have a mount-ing flange that bolts semi-perma-nently to the bench. The alternative attachment on some smaller vises is a screw clamp. The advantage of clamp mounting is that the vise can be removed when space is at a pre-mium. The disadvantage is that, if you need to rotate an item in it (for example, when removing a freewheel) tremendous torque can be imposed on the mounting, with the risk that it could work loose. In fact, if care is not taken when clamping the vise in the first place, it can come right off the bench while you are in mid-strain.

Because of this danger, I prefer to mount my bench vise using nuts and bolts. If you have opted for a folding workbench, but wish to avoid drilling through its top when mounting your vise, make a simple top adapter from a suitably sized piece of plywood (preferably smooth-faced), and bet-ween ½in. and ⅝in. thick. Firmly screw a 2in. x 1in. batten to the underside. Make the top adapter somewhat larger than the folding workbench top if you wish to give yourself a greater working area. For stability this top should not extend more than about 3in. or so on either side. A depth measurement (front to back) of around 16in. is perfectly practical. I have covered my extending top with a piece of rubber matting, stuck down with impact adhesive, to pro-tect the surface. This top adapter is also the perfect site for mounting a drill stand.

Place the top adapter on top of the folding workbench; the batten under-neath is held firmly in place by the workbench's clamping action. The

HOME WORKSHOP

adapter can be removed quickly and easily when you need to mount the workstand in the Workmate.

Power drill/driver
If you can afford it, a middle-priced cordless electric power drill/driver is a versatile asset. As a power driver for screwdrivers, Allen wrenches and sockets you will find it a boon. It will reduce damage to the flats on nuts and bolts, and to the sockets in Allen screws (damage to these is almost inevitable when you use hand tools over a period of time, unless great care is taken). A cordless drill/driver will also speed up numerous bicycle maintenance tasks, especially if, as I recommend, you routinely fit Nyloc nuts wherever possible on your bicycle. As a drill for making holes, for wire brushing, and for a range of other tasks, a cordless drill/driver of this kind will serve practically all your requirements.

A more expensive, but even more versatile choice is to buy an AC heavy duty drill combined with a variable-torque power screwdriver. A wider range of jobs can be tackled with an AC drill when you eventually progress to customizing and repair tasks.

A variable-torque power screwdriver, used with a magnetic chuck adapter, can be used with all the common Allen bits, screwdriver bits and sockets. The screwdriver's size allows good access to most places on a bicycle, but if not, a shaft extension can be fitted quickly and easily.

Drill bits
To complete your power drill set, you will need some drill bits, as well as a few other accessories. A set of top-quality drill bits should feature, at a minimum, a range of sizes from ⅛in. to ¼in. in ¹⁄₃₂in. increments. A range from ¹⁄₁₆in. to ⅜in. is preferable, however. It is best to purchase a complete set with its own holder. Add ¹¹⁄₆₄in., ⁷⁄₃₂in., and ⁹⁄₃₂in. drill bits for drilling holes to be threaded.

As well as a range of drill bits, some rotary wire brushes in a variety of sizes and shapes are really useful (and time-saving) for removing rust or old paint. (Also, remember to buy some protective eyewear, because the little wire bristles on rotary brushes tend to fly off in all directions when the brush is being used.)

A flexible drive extension will allow the wire brush to reach places which are inaccessible with the drill, for example when cleaning out the seat and steerer tubes.

Finally, the Allen wrench bits and sockets in the pistol-grip multi-tool, (which is mentioned later), are ideal for use with a cordless electric drill, preferably with a ¼in. hexagonal socket chuck adapter, which allows you to make quick bit swaps.

It is now possible to buy a wide range of driver bits in the ¼in. hexagonal socket standard. These are most commonly available in boxed sets with their own hand driver – usually a ratchet driver. Such sets feature numerous types of screwdriver bit, but make sure that the Allen bits and sockets are in metric sizes. For use as driver bits, sockets require a hexagon-to-square adapter, and one of these is nearly always included in boxed sets. However, if you decide to buy your ¼in. drive tools separately, make sure you obtain a hexagon-to-square adapter as well.

▲ If funds are limited, a cordless electric drill with a choice of bits is the best option. With a quarter-inch chuck adapter, the drill can be used with the whole range of Allen wrench bits and sockets.

Equivalent drill sizes	English	Metric
	³⁄₆₄in.	1mm
	⁵⁄₆₄in.	2mm
	⅛in.	3mm
	⁵⁄₃₂in.	4mm
	¹³⁄₆₄in.	5mm
	¹⁵⁄₆₄in.	6mm
	⁹⁄₃₂in.	7mm
	⁵⁄₁₆in.	8mm
	²³⁄₆₄in.	9mm
	²⁵⁄₆₄in.	10mm

Hand tools
You will need a good set of wrenches and Allen wrenches, in metric sizes, which is now becoming the standard on most bicycles.

Wrenches
There is no substitute for a complete set of good-quality wrenches. Ideally you should get combination wrenches (that is, they should be open at one end and with a ring at the other; both ends should be of the same size). The best wrenches are made from forged chrome vanadium. As a minimum, buy a range of sizes from 8mm to 17mm, in 1mm increments. Although 16mm and 17mm

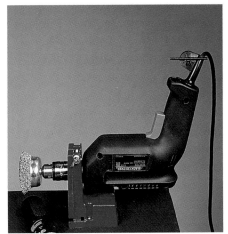

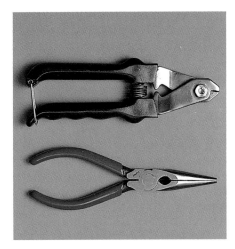

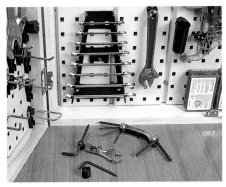

▼ Pliers often come with a wire cutter in the pivot and a cable cutter in the jaws. The former is suitable for cutting control wires, while the latter should only be used for cable casings.

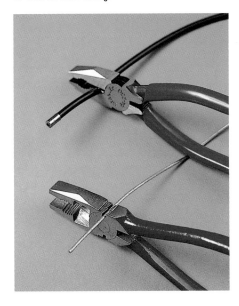

▲ A much wider range of jobs can be tackled with an AC electric drill — especially when a variable-torque power screwdriver (above, left) is used with Allen wrenches, screwdriver bits and sockets.

◄ There is no substitute for a complete set of wrenches, complemented by a good-sized adjustable wrench. A folding set of Allen wrenches does not always include the 2.5mm size. The Cool Tool provides a range of quality tools all in one; it is a good option when funds are short, as will probably be the case when you first set up your workshop.

▲ A pair of long-nose pliers combined with a pair of special wire cutters makes a more versatile, if more expensive, option than standard combination pliers for bicycle maintenance.

nuts and bolts are very rarely featured on bicycles, these sizes are still worth having in your set if you can afford to buy them.

There will also be some occasions when you need two wrenches of the same size. Here, for the sake of economy, a medium-sized 8in. adjustable wrench will be all you need to get by.

If you decide to get a second set of wrenches, buy the type which is open-ended at both ends. Try to get wrenches which have a 1mm difference between each end; this will give you a set comprising one each of 8/9mm, 10/11mm, 12/13mm and 14/15mm.

Allen wrenches
Your set of Allen wrenches should be of very good quality; if they are not, they will turn within the socket, and so will round off the flats of the key, or of the socket, or of both. Further-

more, poor quality Allen wrenches will simply twist when you try to undo a particularly stubborn screw. Ideally, you will need a range of sizes from 2mm to 6mm, again in 1mm increments; a set of these can be bought from bicycle stores in the style of a clasp knife – each Allen wrench folds from a handle, which gives you better purchase if a screw proves stiff to undo. Some adjusters feature a 2.5mm Allen wrench, so check to see if you will need this size. If it is not included in the clasp set, buy one separately. If Allen wrenches are engraved with the letters CRO-MO, this usually shows you that they are of good quality.

Multi-tools
A most useful tool is a pistol-grip ratchet driver. This comes with a range of screwdriver and Allen bits, as well as sockets, which are all stored in a molded insert which fits into the handle. The pistol-grip screwdriver will not only serve in the workshop, but can be used in your emergency kit (which you should carry with you on your bicycle). The bits and sockets are, as has been mentioned above, ideal for use with a power screwdriver.

HOME WORKSHOP

Another multi-tool which is made to a sufficiently high standard to warrant a place in your workshop is a Cool Tool. It features an adjustable wrench for use on bearing cones, 4mm, 5mm and 6mm Allen wrenches, a Phillips screwdriver, a chain tool and a crank bolt socket wrench.

Combination pliers
A pair of pliers will sometimes include a wire cutter in its pivot, as well as a cable cutter in its jaws. The cable cutter is only suitable for cutting control cable casings. When cutting cable inner wires, it is important to achieve a clean cut to prevent the wire from fraying. For both of these cutters to be effective, the pliers must be of the best quality.

If you cannot find such a pair of pliers, opt for a combined set comprising a pair of special brake wire cutters and a pair of long-nose pliers, which can reach less accessible places and handle small parts more delicately. Although long-nose pliers never feature wire cutters, they do usually have a cable cutter. This combination is more expensive, but much more versatile. For example, if you grind or file the ends of the pliers into pins, they also do quite nicely as a substitute pin wrench.

Screwdrivers
Purchase a pair of high-quality long-shafted screwdrivers; one should be of the slotted type, the other a Phillips screwdriver. Long-shafted screwdrivers provide extra purchase for stubborn screws and allow access to those which are difficult to reach. You can also sometimes hold the screwdriver by the shaft, quite near the head, to spin it, which speeds up the removal of long screws.

Visegrip pliers
A pair of visegrip pliers can be used to grip small items that, while being worked on, are awkward to hold in the fingers. Stubborn nuts can also be gripped and undone with them,

and they can be made to exert enhanced pressure, which makes them valuable for many tasks.

Hacksaw
To cut excess from bolts, and for a variety of metal and plastic sawing jobs, a small hacksaw of the best quality is quite adequate.

Hammers
You will need two hammers: a light ¾lb ball peen hammer (for sharp impact), and a rubber-headed hammer for when the blow needs to be

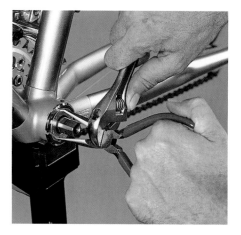

▼ Long-shafted screwdrivers give good accessibility. Visegrip pliers can also grip stubborn bolts and nuts. A small hacksaw can cut most materials. Swiss files, with an interchangeable handle, are inexpensive. For cleaning as you work: a small wire brush and a paintbrush. The toothbrush can simply be recycled from the bathroom.

▲ If using long-nose pliers as a pin wrench, support them with an adjustable wrench across the legs, as shown. One hand pushes the ends into the pin holes, while the other hand turns the adjustable wrench. Carry out this operation carefully to avoid twisting the pivot on the pliers, or damaging the pinholes in the bearing you are adjusting.

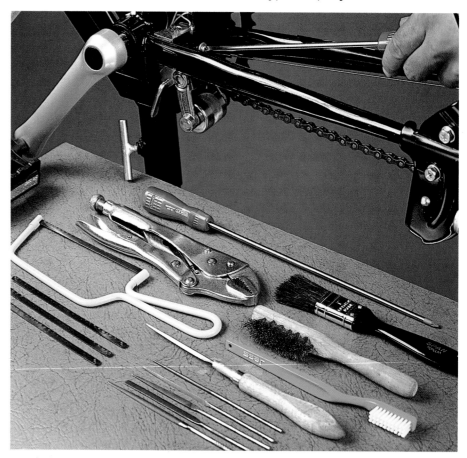

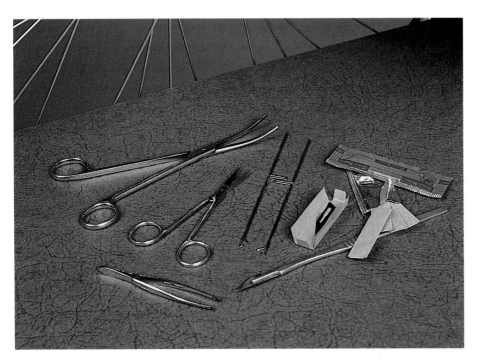

◀ For handling small items, such as individual ball bearings, surgical instruments are ideal. I frequently use a pair of pointed tweezers, a small pair of scissors, a pair of forceps, a clasp-hook and a scalpel with replaceable blades.

softened. The latter can be bought from outdoor stores. More sophisticated, and more expensive, soft-faced hammers made from a special plastic material, or copper, can be bought, but there is really no need to go for such high quality.

A range of drifts and punches should be acquired. Drifts are simply lengths of metal rod or tube, which can be used with a hammer to achieve a pinpoint blow. The drift/hammer combination can also substitute for a C wrench on the bottom bracket lockring. If a sharp impact is required, then use a 6in. length of ⅜in. diameter chrome molybdenum rod (generally known as 'cro-mo'). Thinner, thicker, longer and shorter pieces of this, or a similar type of hardened steel alloy, will prove their usefulness. They can be acquired from hardware scrap. If you need something to give a softer impact, use some pieces of copper rod or tube, such as remnants of plumbers' tube, which is very easy to obtain. Lengths of hardwood dowel are also useful for softening a hammer blow, though they are too thick for delicate work.

Files
It is unlikely that you will need to do any substantial filing. Nevertheless, there is occasionally a need to clean up a thread, or relieve a pivot. For these purposes a set of tiny Swiss files are a cheap purchase. These are often available in sets, in a wide range of shapes, and they usually have an interchangeable handle. As you gain confidence as a mechanic, larger files will make worthwhile additions to your tool set. Make sure these are of good quality, otherwise you will spend a lot of time filing and getting nowhere. Also learn how to use a file correctly – this is important both to prevent accidents, and damage to the item you are working on.

Surgical instruments
For handling small items, such as individual ball bearings, surgical instruments are ideal. I use a pair of pointed tweezers, a pair of forceps, a clasp-hook and a scalpel with replaceable blades. Such items are not generally available; however, you may find them either in specialist model stores or at a drug store.

Taps and dies
Simply for cleaning dirty or damaged internal (female) threads in nuts and components, a set of M5, M6 and M8 taps will suffice. From time to time, you may find the taps useful for actually cutting a thread in a hole. To drill the correct diameter hole for threading, you will need corresponding drill bits of ¹¹⁄₆₄in., ⁷⁄₃₂in., and ⁹⁄₃₂in. respectively, and a tap wrench is important here to aid accurate, square cutting. When cutting a thread, start with a few full turns to begin the thread, then make only half-turns, reversing the tap a quarter-turn for each half-turn forward, to clear the cutting edge and prevent burrs from building up. Continue to cut the thread with a half-turn forward, quarter-turn back, and so on until the job is completed.

The corresponding M5, M6 and M8 dies are also useful for dressing threads on bolts. You will rarely need to cut a male thread, so inexpensive dies are fine for this purpose.

Cleaning brushes
For precision cleaning of assemblies and components as you work, have available in your maintenance kit a stiff 1in. paintbrush, a toothbrush and a small wire brush.

Tool storage
Storing your workshop tools can present problems if you do not have a permanent workshop, and you need to pack them away for storage when they are not in use. They will need to be secure, and to be arranged for maximum convenience.

Despite years of searching, I have yet to discover a suitable commercially available storage cupboard, so I designed and made my own. The principle behind the design means

HOME WORKSHOP

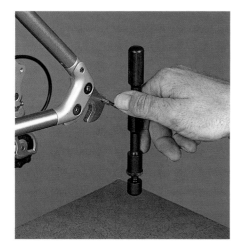

▲ Use a tap not just to clean threads, but also to cut a thread in a plain hole of the correct diameter. The tap wrench makes it easier to hold the tap square, but an adjustable wrench will do the job.

Drill hole size	Tap size
$^3/_{16}$ in.	M5
$^7/_{32}$ in.	M6
$^9/_{32}$ in.	M8

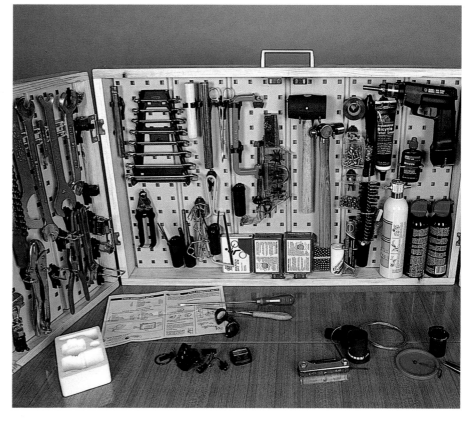

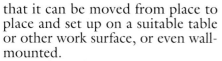

▲ Inside the tool storage cupboard your tools should be conveniently arranged. Magnetic tool racks (left hand panel, at top) are very convenient, as are these perforated panels designed for a wide range of special clip-in hooks and brackets. You can buy the panels at many hardware stores.

▼ A metal hammer is necessary for a sharp impact, but be sure to use a drift to avoid damaging the surrounding area. The hammer and drift combination can also substitute for a C wrench on the bottom bracket lockring. For a softer blow, use a wooden drift or a rubber-headed hammer.

that it can be moved from place to place and set up on a suitable table or other work surface, or even wall-mounted.

Another advantage with building your own cupboard is that it can be made to exactly your requirements. You may prefer to make a large cupboard, in which you can keep as many of your workshop items as possible, thus simplifying any pack-away operation (although the weight of the packed cupboard may make transportation a little more difficult). Alternatively, you may prefer to make two smaller cupboards, which should be easier to move.

There is no one way to design and build this cupboard. You can either construct it yourself using the simplest of techniques and tools; or you could commission a local cabinet maker to produce a substantial and well-designed cupboard which will last a lifetime.

Inside the tool-storage cupboard your tools should be arranged so that you can select the right tool when you need it. Hang each tool from a hook, or secure them with clips. Whatever method you choose, bear in mind that the panel material you use to make the cupboard may not be thick enough to screw into. If this is the case you can use rivets or machine screws, nuts and washers. Magnetic tool racks are very convenient, because the tools don't have to be put back in exactly the allotted place every time – but make sure that the magnetism is strong enough to hold your heaviest tools.

The ideal way of arranging your

tools inside the cupboard is by installing pre-drilled panels which have regular perforations to accept a wide range of special clip-in hooks and brackets. It is possible to cut these panels to size, or you can build the cupboard around the manufacturer's standard sizes. The big advantage of this system is that the hooks and brackets can be moved around, and added to, as the number of your workshop tools increase, or change in type.

By fitting a carrying handle onto the tool storage cupboard, you will make it easier to carry from place to place; a shoulder strap may also be handy. Make sure that the latches you use will keep the cupboard securely closed in transit.

Apart from the storage of most of your workshop tools, you must allow

▼ Choose a toolbox large enough to store all your tools, spare parts and materials. This one has partitioned drawers for storing small parts and spare parts and is fitted with casters, making it very much easier to move around when loaded.

a space for your cordless drill (which may have its own mounting bracket) close to an electric socket so that the drill can be on almost constant charge. If you keep the rechargeable drills or drivers inside the storage cupboard itself, you could plan it so that they can be charged while inside, with the wire routed to the charger plugged into a nearby socket.

Toolbox
If the tool storage cupboard design is not suitable for your purposes, choose a toolbox large enough to store all your tools, spare parts and other materials.

The drawback of a toolbox is that all your tools are in one compartment – with the one you want, it seems, always at the bottom. One solution is to get a toolbox which has a number of trays or drawers. By keeping your tools in a particular place within the toolbox, you will avoid the perennial 'bottom of the box' problem. Store the most frequently used tools conveniently at hand in the top trays.

Tool care
Over a lifetime, you will probably buy several bicycles – but, with care, you will only ever need one set of workshop tools and equipment. So, regard tools as a long-term investment. If you look after your tools, they will be giving good service long after you have no more use for them.

Most tools require very little routine maintenance; simply keep them clean and lubricate them regularly where necessary. But more importantly, use them with care, since most damage and wear to tools is caused by carelessness. Be sure to use the right tool for the task in hand: a wrench that fits the nut exactly, an Allen wrench that fits the socket, and so on.

Perhaps the most important rule in tool care is to never lend your tools to anyone, ever. If someone does ask to borrow your tools, it may well be better for you to offer to fix their bicycle yourself. Another diplomatic solution is to have a second set of cheaper, and less favored tools for lending out. (This is a particularly handy strategy for those with families when, with the best will in the world, not every member understands the need for reliable tools.) In the meantime, buy a sturdy lock for the number one set.

Bits box
The 'bits box' cannot be bought: it is a collection of nuts, bolts, brackets and any pieces of material that you have saved with the idea that they may, conceivably, be useful one day. The collection of 'bits' is accumulated by never throwing away anything that could be useful. For example, when you change or upgrade items on your bicycle, all nuts, bolts, washers and brackets should be removed from the worn-out or damaged component assemblies and saved, and the damaged parts disposed of. The collection can be augmented with items you find elsewhere, such as pieces of material procured from hardware scrap. The bits box itself, meanwhile,

should be made of metal or molded plastic. The contents of the box should be sprayed lightly with rust inhibitor from time to time.

When it comes to finding small parts in the bits box – such as that little tanged washer you know is in there – it is easier if the contents can be spread out and sorted through on a large metal tray. One of the trays you normally use for cleaning will be fine for this. From time to time, it is also worthwhile sorting through everything you have collected and classifying all the bits and pieces.

Air

To pump up tires, you will need a source of air. An ordinary, inexpensive bicycle pump will suffice until you find yourself more involved in bicycle maintenance, when a special foot pump could be purchased. These are very high capacity air pumps, which have a vertical air chamber operated by means of a T-handled plunger. The body of the pump is stabilized by means of two feet at the base. The operator stands on these, then, with both hands on the T-handle, pumps away. Foot pumps often feature a built-in pressure gauge to ensure that you don't over-inflate the tire and so damage it.

Rechargeable aerosol

Whatever your air supply, whether it be a hand pump or compressor, you can also use it to charge up rechargeable aerosol canisters. These then provide a source of high-pressure air for air-blast cleaning of components when you are working on them. A rechargeable aerosol is environmentally sound and can be used time and time again, either with air for cleaning as described here, or for spraying thin fluids such as degreaser, lubricant, paint and so on.

Spare parts and consumables

A workshop should not only contain tools, but also a stock of spare parts for your bicycle, and for any other

▲ The bits box will prove its value time and again. Small parts are easier to find if they are spread out and sorted on a large metal tray. Spray the contents with a rust inhibitor every so often.

▲ Recycle your old spokes by making a selection of hooks and retainers of all shapes and sizes. Design some carefully for specific purposes and keep them as a permanent part of the workshop.

bicycles you are looking after as well. The list of spare parts can really be as long as you wish, provided you have the space to store them all. Whatever, make sure you always have the essentials, and that they are of the correct size and type to fit the bicycles you are in charge of.

Consumables, meanwhile, are those materials that get used up while you work on your bicycle, such as cleaning fluids, adhesives, tapes, lubricants and so on.

Lubrication technology is a real maze, with different manufacturers and experts making complicated, and sometimes contradictory, claims for their products. The basic choice is between the traditional oil-based lubricants and the more recently developed (and more expensive) synthetic lubrication systems.

In my role as a professional cyclist and writer, I have tested many different lubricants at different times on each of my bicycles. I have concluded that, depending on your require-

▶ Your air supply can be used for filling rechargeable aerosol canisters, which are excellent for air-blast cleaning and for spraying thin fluids such as degreaser, lubricant, paint and so on.

ments, there seems to be room for both types – but that you should never mix the two on the same bicycle, as the additives used by one manufacturer may not be compatible with those used by another. Decide on the type of lubrication and cleaning system that will suit your needs, and use that one only.

The latest developments in synthetic lubricants mean that they are

beginning to supersede the more traditional petroleum oils. I am much attracted by the new synthetic lubrication systems which have been formulated specifically for bicycles. These are compatible within the system, and offer a range of lubricants, greases, polishes, cleaning fluids, degreasers, and so on.

Cleaning rags
Always keep a good stock of cleaning rags for when you are working on your bicycle. Store them according to how contaminated they are; for example, clean, soiled and dirty. Sometimes it makes good sense to clean a dirty part first using a dirty rag – this saves you from spoiling a clean one. Once you have progressed to the reassembly stage, you should always use clean rags.

Recycling bicycle parts
Never throw away old spokes – they are easy to store and take up very little room in your workshop. With a pair of pliers, or using your hands, you can shape them into double-ended hooks, or S hooks. If you have a regular use for one of these hooks, (for example to relieve tension in the chain by hooking up the rear derailleur), then get the design exactly right for your bicycle and regard the hook as one of your tools. Other designs of S hook are required occa-

▲ A minimum spare parts stock would contain all of the following items:
• A selection of nuts, bolts and washers
• Two inner tubes
• Spare valves
• A complete set of control inner wires

• Bulbs and batteries for lights
• One complete chain
• A selection of loose ball bearings
• A pair of brake blocks
• Spare key for lock and/or alarm
• Spare pulley wheel set

▼ Always have on hand a number of materials for use in maintenance and for the inevitable repairs:
• PVC adhesive tape
• Plumbers' Teflon tape (for repairing a stripped thread temporarily)
• Thread adhesive
• Degreaser spray

• General purpose superglue
• Contact cement
• Strips of emery cloth
• Metal polish
• Talcum powder
• Rubber cement
• Puncture patches
• Plastic cable ties
• Lubes and cleaners

sionally on a one-off basis, but it is still worth keeping these in a special place in case you need them again.

Old inner tubes are also worth keeping: they can be cut into rubber bands using a pair of scissors. The wider the band, the stronger and less elastic it is. Cut several bands of differing widths at one go and keep them ready for use. For example, bands can be used over the handlebar and brake lever to hold the brake on – and, if left in that position, they can act as parking brakes. Another use for lengths of old inner tube is to roll one over the headset cups when you are undertaking an overhaul. When you have finished, they can be rolled down to provide an excellent water seal for the bearings.

Conclusion
The workshop I have described here, although fairly basic, is in fact sufficiently versatile to enable you successfully to carry out a wide range of repairs – once you have acquired the necessary skills by regularly doing your own maintenance on your bicycle. However, over time you will certainly want to add further tools to your set – especially if you advance on to customizing and repair jobs – and through experience you will get to know which ones will be useful specifically to you. This is when your workshop will become truly established.

CLEANING

Generally, if you have the time, cleaning your bicycle before any checks are carried out makes the routine that much more easy and effective. However, cleaning before the four- to six-week routine is essential.

A garden hose makes rinsing more convenient, effective and speedy. It is best to fit a nozzle to the hose, which does not significantly increase the risk of water penetrating the bearing. Do not use a pressure washer in case it forces water into the bearings.

There are two approaches to cleaning a bicycle; which one you take depends on what you use your bicycle for. A muddy mountain bicycle will need to be cleaned immediately after a ride, whereas a bicycle used predominantly on the road will require a good cleaning every four to six weeks only.

Muddy mountain bike
Whether or not you plan to go through a check routine, if your bicycle is very muddy after a ride it should be washed down while the mud is still fresh. (If the mud is left to harden, and it contains salt, it will have a corrosive effect.)

If you do not intend to check your bicycle over, then it should be washed in water only, preferably using a garden hose and a soft brush. The chain may be left in place. After you have rinsed all the mud away, you can use a water-displacing lubricant spray on the chain and on all pivoting parts – you don't need to wait for the bicycle to dry. Be careful to avoid getting any of the spray onto either the braking surface of the rims, or on the brake blocks.

You may be tempted to use one of the high-pressure washing hoses that are available at many garages. This is certainly a very quick and effective method of cleaning your bicycle, but unless extreme caution is taken there is the likelihood that the water, flowing as it does at very high pressure, will penetrate right into the bearings. You will then have to strip down and regrease the bicycle.

Normal cleaning routine
Cleaning your bicycle is a regular routine, and each part of the operation should be carried out in the same order each time. Follow the steps set out here.

Stand your bicycle upright
It is always best to clean your bicycle when it is upright, because if it is upside-down, water can penetrate into the headset bearings. In some cases, it may also get inside the frame tubes through the little blow-holes left by the manufacturing process. Lean your bicycle against a wall if you do not have any form of stand, and

▲ Items you will need to clean your bicycle:
- Small bicycle stand
- Chain tool
- Metal tray
- 1in. paintbrush
- Water-soluble degreaser
- Garden hose
- Bucket of hot water
- Teaspoon of vinegar
- Liquid detergent
- Soft brush
- Towel

use inner tube rubber bands to hold the brakes on and prevent the bicycle from moving. Otherwise, put your bicycle onto a bicycle stand and

▲ Use the edge of a towel to clean between the sprockets. If the build-up of muck is too solid, use a small screwdriver to break it up first.

▼ When pouring degreaser from a gallon can, although it seems illogical, tilt the can with the spout uppermost to allow air into the can.

▲ In winter, and if you ride in the city, use water-soluble degreaser around your brakes. Clean the brakes thoroughly with water afterwards.

make sure that it is stable and that it will not fall over easily. Here again you can use inner tube rubber bands to secure the front brake.

Pour degreaser into a tray
It is most economical to buy degreaser by the gallon can. Always wear safety glasses when pouring, in case degreaser splashes into your eyes. To protect the skin on your hands, wear chemical-resistant gloves. (Regular rubber gloves will also protect your hands, but they will be attacked by the degreaser in a relatively short time and will have to be discarded after only one cleaning.) Only half-fill the metal tray with the degreaser to avoid spillage.

Remove the chain
Refer to page 46 for details of how to do this. When you have removed the chain, put it into the tray of degreaser to soak.

Degreasing
Use a regular 1in. paintbrush to brush degreasing fluid from the tray

into the greasy, oily areas: that is, over and between the freewheel sprockets, around the jockey wheels and cage, and over the teeth of the chainrings. In winter weather, especially if you ride in the city, the rims and around the brakes should be treated with degreaser, too. Again, while doing this be very careful to avoid getting any splashes in your eyes, and use the degreaser sparingly.

Once you have brushed the degreaser over the greasy parts with the paintbrush, use a stiffer brush to work on any particularly stubborn grime. Leave the degreaser for some minutes to penetrate the grease and put the tray to one side, so that it will not get sprayed with water while you continue cleaning.

Washing
Fill your bucket with hot water, and add some liquid detergent and a teaspoon of vinegar to it. The vinegar acts as a mild degreaser, but it is not neutralized by the water. Using the larger brush, slosh the soapy water all over the bicycle and use the brush vigorously to clear away any grime. Pay particular attention to the areas on which you have used de-greaser. You can use the paintbrush with the soapy water to get into difficult places, such as the body of wheel hubs, but do not now put the paintbrush back into the degreaser. Avoid rubbing soapy water into the bearings; if these areas need special cleaning, it can be done at the check stage, using a toothbrush.

Rinsing
Using as much clean water as necessary, rinse the bicycle thoroughly. Once you are satisfied that all the soap and degreaser have been washed away, you can shake off much of the water by bouncing your bicycle on its tires. Finally, go over the entire bicycle with a dry towel, paying particular attention to the areas where the cleaning has not been totally effective.

Your bicycle is now ready for a check or service routine, or for dismantling for overhaul.

DISMANTLING

When the time for an overhaul arrives, you will need to dismantle your bicycle. The dismantling process leads directly on from the cleaning detailed in the previous section. We can now start work with a clean bicycle, mounted on the workstand. Next the bicycle will be completely dismantled in preparation for the cleaning of the smaller assemblies and parts.

It is a good idea to prepare for this operation by gathering a collection of small cardboard boxes (you can get them from a supermarket) or stacking molded plastic containers. As you remove each assembly or group of components from your bicycle, keep them together in one of the boxes while they await cleaning and overhaul.

Refer to the maintenance pages for details of how to remove each part or assembly.

Chain
- The chain will have already been removed from the bicycle and set aside ready for cleaning.

Wheels
- Remove the wheels first, because they can obstruct access to other assemblies.
- You may remove the freewheel at this stage and put it into the transmission parts box.
- Remove the tires, inner tubes and rim tapes. Hang these, with the wheels, out of the way.

Accessories
- Remove all lighting equipment, together with any wiring, and put it all together in a separate box.
- Remove the rack and hang it out of the way.
- Remove the fenders and hang these out of the way.
- Remove the bottle cages, but refit the screws in the frame, to act as plugs.
- Remove any other accessories you may have, such as a computer.

Control cables
- Disconnect and remove each con-trol cable in turn and wind it for storage.
- Make sure the ferrules are replaced in the right order.
- If you are not sure which cable is which, label each one before disconnecting it.
- Store the brake cables in the box with the brake calipers, and the gear cables with all the other transmission parts.

Handlebars
- Disconnect the cables from the handlebar assembly, and remove the whole assembly by the handlebar stem, complete with grips, brake levers and gear shifters.
- Hang the assembly out of the way.

Saddle and seat post
- Remove the saddle and seat post together. You can leave the quick-release in place if you wish.
- Stuff a piece of clean rag down the saddle hole, making sure there is a tail hanging out so you can retrieve the rag later.

Brakes
- Remove the calipers.
- If your calipers have brazed-on bosses, then use a small length of wire to secure the mounting bolt to the assembly so that you do not loose it.

Pedals
- There is no need to remove the pedals from the cranks to overhaul them, but if you choose to, now is the time to do it.

Crankset
- Remove the cranks.
- Remove the bottom bracket bearings and put these in a container of degreaser to soak.

Gears
- Remove the rear derailleur – there is no need to remove the front derailleur, but you can if you wish to be very thorough.

Forks
- Remove the headset bearings and put these in a container of degreaser to soak.
- The forks are removed with the headset.

Cleaning small parts
The cleaning of your bicycle in preparation for an overhaul must be scrupulous and complete. It is very important that all the parts are as clean as possible when you are regreasing bearings to prevent contaminants from getting into the bearing before you begin reassembly.

Several places will remain affected by caked-on grime after your quick clean, and all the internal bearings must be cleaned to remove the old grease, which will have become contaminated with use. Several solvents are available on the market which are designed to break down these substances. Kerosene is a popular and cheap cleaning fluid for bicycle parts, but it contains a lot of water and leaves residues which have to be removed, whereas naphtha is more refined and doesn't smell as bad. Petroleum-based lighter fluid, used in very small quantities, is an excel-

▼ If you choose to recycle your degreaser, first allow the used fluid to settle in the container. Then use a siphon pump to siphon off the clean degreaser once all the solids have settled to the bottom. Afterwards, the pump should be cleaned thoroughly by running water through it; allow it to dry before using it again. This prevents the degreaser from attacking any of the seals in the pump mechanism.

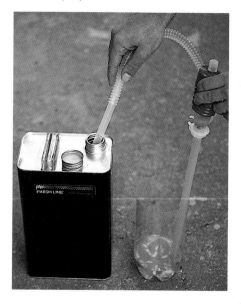

▲ When rinsing items in water after using degreaser, you will notice that the liquid becomes milky. This milky appearance indicates that the degreaser is being neutralized by the water.

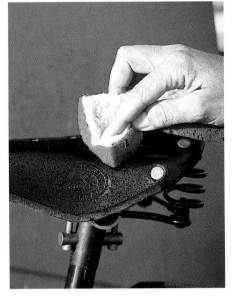

▲ A dirty leather saddle must not be cleaned with anything other than saddle soap and water. After cleaning, be sure to dress the saddle with the correct cream. Cover the saddle when washing the bicycle.

If you are working with a component that has internal bearings or pivots which you do not plan to dismantle – for example, a quick-release indexed shift lever, derailleur or freewheel – be careful to prevent degreaser penetrating them.

After you have completed the initial cleaning of an assembly or component with degreaser, the items should be cleaned again in slightly soapy water. After that, they should be completely rinsed in clean water. If any dirt remains once you have dried the component with a rag, use some lighter fluid or naphtha and a small wire brush to remove it, if necessary. Pivoting assemblies can be sprayed with electricians' switch-cleaner to drive out all water before you lubricate them again.

It is best not to clean parts made of rubber, such as the tires, handlebar grips and brake blocks, with degreaser. Although it should not damage them so long as the degreaser is washed off quickly, exposure over a longer period of time may cause the rubber to decay.

Lighting equipment should never be cleaned with degreaser and water, because these substances will affect the electric contacts. Clean the contacts with emery cloth if necessary.

lent cleaner both because it is highly refined and because it evaporates quickly, leaving virtually no residue. This makes it ideal for such jobs as fitting handlebar grips, where it cleans, lubricates, and then conveniently evaporates.

The most convenient and effective product for cleaning small parts, however, is one of the several commercial water-soluble degreasers. Remember that, when handling degreaser, you should always wear safety glasses to prevent the fluid splashing into your eyes. Also, wear chemical-resistant gloves, as advised elsewhere.

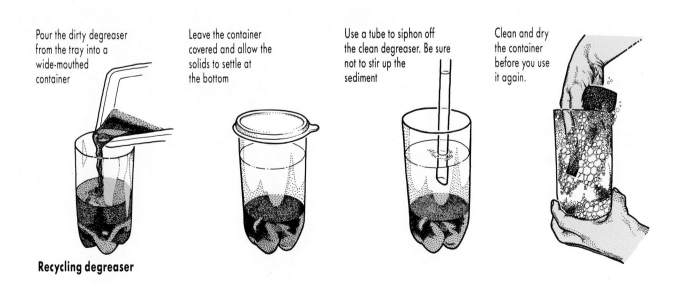

Pour the dirty degreaser from the tray into a wide-mouthed container

Leave the container covered and allow the solids to settle at the bottom

Use a tube to siphon off the clean degreaser. Be sure not to stir up the sediment

Clean and dry the container before you use it again.

Recycling degreaser

WEEKLY CHECK

It is most worthwhile setting aside a little time each week to get your bicycle onto the workstand, both to check it over and to make those small adjustments that will keep it running efficiently at all times.

In snowy winter weather, when road salt will be in evidence, you should also clean your bicycle at this weekly check, because of the highly corrosive effect of road salt. However, for most of the year it will not be necessary to clean your bicycle each time: the weekly check is intended to be as quick as possible.

While riding during the week, you may have become aware of a problem, usually by hearing something that's not quite right – a gear not meshing or a creak here, a rattle there. It is surprising how easily threaded items can work loose, sometimes quite suddenly, and this is not always because they have been tightened carelessly. It is important to check and correct these problems at this time, rather than leave them until the service routine. Unless you have the time, avoid the temptation of attempting jobs that are best left until you complete a full service routine.

If you undertake this check regularly, it is unlikely that it will be necessary to do anything other than make adjustments, and you will rarely need to repair your bicycle.

You may find it useful to take a photocopy of the checklist and to mount it on some cardboard. Display it in the workshop so you can refer to it as you go through the routine. Also consider making reminder notes about your own bicycle where it differs from the one used as an example in this diagram.

In the maintenance section you will find recommendations for what to check on each individual area of your bicycle, followed with advice on how to adjust it so that it is operating efficiently. The diagram (right) shows what pages you should refer to as you work your way down the checklist given in the right-hand column.

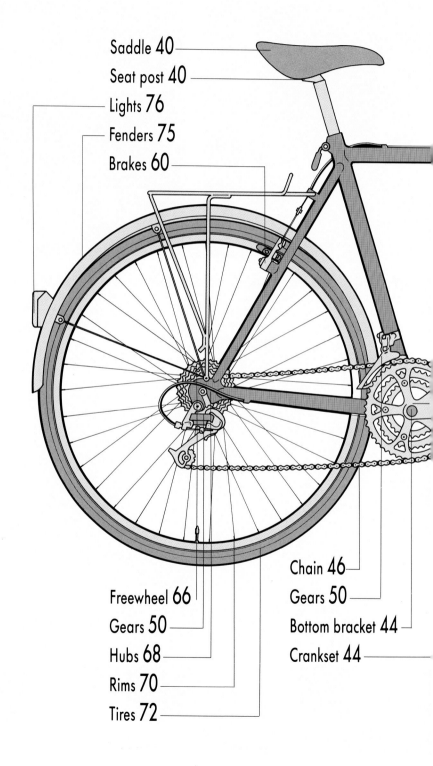

Saddle 40
Seat post 40
Lights 76
Fenders 75
Brakes 60

Freewheel 66
Gears 50
Hubs 68
Rims 70
Tires 72

Chain 46
Gears 50
Bottom bracket 44
Crankset 44

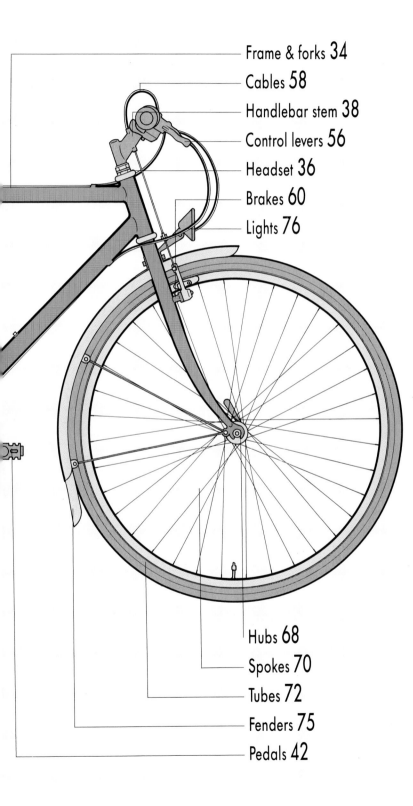

Frame & forks **34**

Cables **58**

Handlebar stem **38**

Control levers **56**

Headset **36**

Brakes **60**

Lights **76**

Hubs **68**

Spokes **70**

Tubes **72**

Fenders **75**

Pedals **42**

Chain
- Remove (winter only).
- Clean and dry.
- Check for wear and stiff links.
- Lube ready for refitting.
- Lube only (summer). No need to remove.
- If you are using the rotation method (see pages 48-49), remove the chain at the beginning of the check and replace it with a fresh one when you have finished.

Cleaning
- Clean the bicycle if necessary.

Wheels
- Check spoke tension.
- Check wheel bearings for play.

Tires
- Check for sidewall or tread area splits or other damage.
- Check tire pressure.

Brakes
- Check brake cable adjustment.
- Put a drop of lube into the pivots.

Cables
- Check inner wires for fraying.
- Check casings for kinks or splits.

Bearings
- Check the headset bearings for looseness or tightness.
- Check the bottom bracket bearings for looseness or tightness.
- Check the pedal bearings for looseness or tightness.

Gears
- Check that each gear is engaging properly.
- Put a drop of lube onto each pivot.

Lights
- Check that both the front and rear lights are working.

Fenders
- Check that the stays are not rubbing the tire.

Chain
- Refit (winter only).
- Check for stiff links.

Nuts and bolts
- Check that all nuts and bolts are tight. It is very easy to miss one if you simply go around the bicycle, so make a list and keep it with your tools. Refer to it each time you carry out this check.

REGULAR SERVICE

Every four to six weeks, the regular weekly check should be supplemented by a slightly more thorough one. This should still be relatively quick to complete unless, of course, you find a repair that must be made immediately.

Whatever the season, you should clean the bicycle before you begin the service routine. Be especially thorough with your cleaning in the winter months when roads are salted. Road salt is highly corrosive and will eat into the aluminum alloy components on your bicycle quickly.

It is during this routine that more complicated adjustments should be made; for easy reference the relevant pages of the maintenance section are shown on the center panel. As with the weekly checklist, this page can be photocopied into a larger format and referred to as you run through the routine in your workshop. The check is complete in itself, so you do not need to refer back to the weekly checklist.

At the end of this process, a short test ride is advisable to make sure everything is working properly.

Chain
- Remove the chain.
- Clean and dry.
- Check for wear and stiff links.
- If you are using the rotation method, you will have a fresh chain ready to be refitted at the end of the service.

Cleaning
Before mounting the bicycle on the workstand:
- Clean the bicycle thoroughly.
- Check the headset bearings for looseness or tightness.
- Check frame/wheel alignment.
- Check handlebar alignment.

Wheels
- Check spoke tension.
- Check rim for dents or damage.
- Check wheel for trueness.
- Check wheel bearings for looseness or tightness.
- Remove wheels.

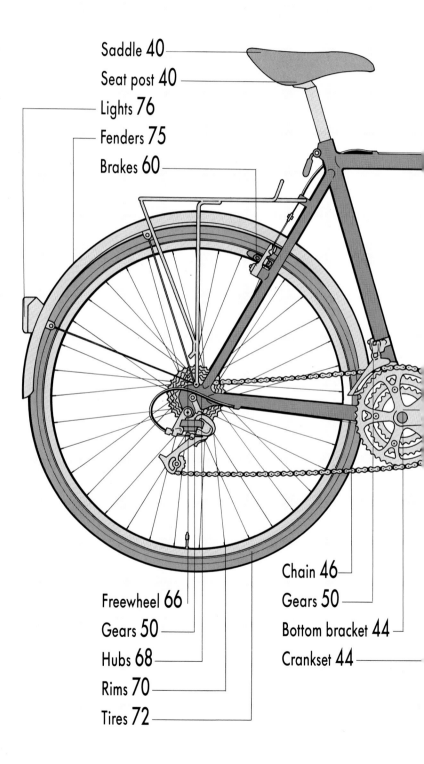

Saddle 40
Seat post 40
Lights 76
Fenders 75
Brakes 60

Freewheel 66
Gears 50
Hubs 68
Rims 70
Tires 72

Chain 46
Gears 50
Bottom bracket 44
Crankset 44

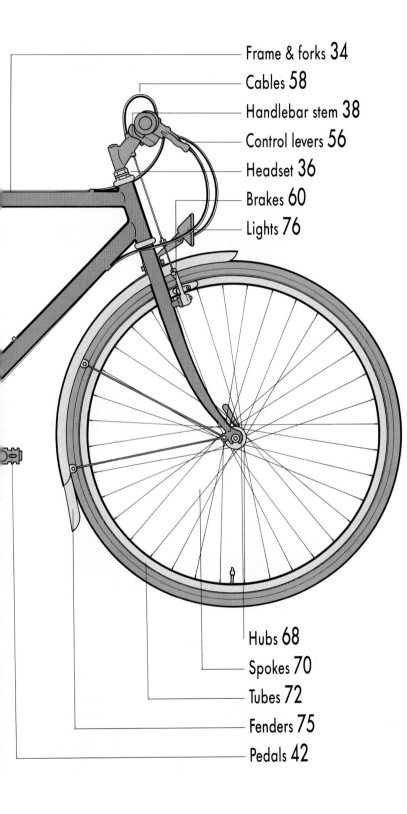

Frame & forks **34**

Cables **58**

Handlebar stem **38**

Control levers **56**

Headset **36**

Brakes **60**

Lights **76**

Hubs **68**

Spokes **70**

Tubes **72**

Fenders **75**

Pedals **42**

Freewheel
- Check for smooth rotation and for any wear.

Tires
- Check for splits.
- Deflate and check for ozone cracks.

Brakes
- Clean and check the brake blocks. Remove the blocks to do this if you wish.

Cables
- Disconnect the cables at each end and check them to make sure that the inner wire slides smoothly within the outer casing.
- Check the inner wires for any signs of fraying.
- Check casings for kinks or splits.
- Reconnect the cables.

Bearings
- Check the bottom bracket bearings for looseness or tightness.
- Check the pedal bearings for looseness or tightness.

Rear derailleur
- Check the pulleys for wear.
- Check all the pivoting parts.
- Check alignment.

Front derailleur
- Check all the pivoting parts.
- Check the throw adjustment.
- Check alignment and position.

Reassembly
- Replace the wheels.
- Reinflate tires.
- Check tire seating.
- Check tire pressure.
- Check and adjust the brake block alignment and toe-out.
- Check brakes for binding.
- Check brake cable adjustment.
- Check rear derailleur throw adjustment.
- Refit the chain.
- Check for any stiff links.
- Check for any bent or misaligned teeth.
- Check gear indexing.
- Check front and rear lights.

Nuts and bolts
- Check that all nuts and bolts are tight, using the same list created for the weekly check.

OVERHAUL ROUTINE

An overhaul should be carried out every six months on any bicycle that is used frequently. In the fall, the bicycle will be prepared for the ravages of the imminent winter weather. Likewise, in spring, the effects of those months of hard weather can be remedied. Even if you rarely use your bicycle, carry out an overhaul every 12 months at least – otherwise the bicycle's condition will deteriorate.

This overhaul could be completed in one day but, realistically, you should allow more time – a weekend is ideal. It is a good idea to do all the cleaning and dismantling on a Friday evening so that any unforeseen requirements can be bought at your local bicycle store on the Saturday. The overhaul can then be completed on the Sunday, in time for a short test ride, which should be undertaken before all the tools are packed away.

Friday evening
• Clean and dismantle the bicycle.
Saturday morning
• Clean and check all parts and components.
Saturday afternoon
• Purchase any replacement parts.
Saturday evening
• Work on parts and components; complete any repairs.
Sunday morning
• Re-assemble the bicycle; make all the necessary adjustments.
Sunday afternoon
• Test ride the bicycle and make any final adjustments.
Sunday evening
• Clean and pack away your tools.

The parts that should be routinely replaced at the overhaul stage should either be held in stock, or bought in advance. Check your bicycle for the correct replacement parts and sizes for the following:
• Ball bearings for all bearings.
• Chain.
• Control cable inner wires.
• Brake blocks.

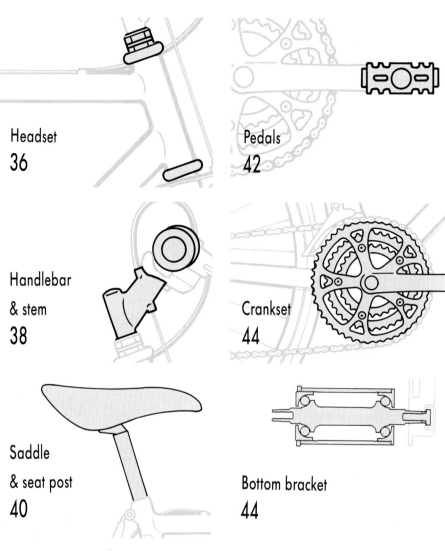

Headset
36

Handlebar
& stem
38

Saddle
& seat post
40

Pedals
42

Crankset
44

Bottom bracket
44

• Derailleur pulleys.
  The following may need to be replaced as well:
• Tires.
• Inner tubes.
• Handlebar grips or tape.

This routine checklist follows on from previous checklists; it is also assumed that the bicycle has been dismantled, so there is no need for you to refer back.

Frame and forks
• Check for cracks and bends.
• Touch-up paintwork.
• Clean inside steerer and seat tubes.

Headset
• Renew ball bearings and regrease.
• Adjust headset.
Handlebar and stem
• Check for scratches and bends.
Saddle and seat post
• Check condition of saddle top.
• Check insert height of seat post and clean the shaft.
Pedals
• Check for bent spindle.
• Dismantle, clean and regrease the bearings.
• Adjust bearings.
Crankset
• Check for buckles.
• Check for misaligned teeth.

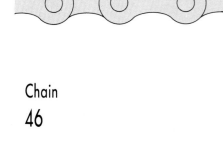

Chain
46

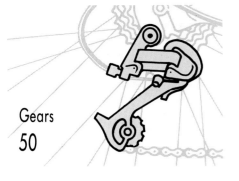

Gears
50

Cables
58

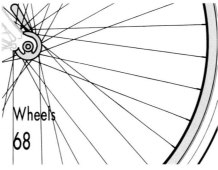

Brakes
60

Wheels
68

Tires
& tubes
72

- Check for tooth wear.
- Check for bent crank.

Bottom bracket
- Dismantle, clean and regrease the bearing.
- Adjust bearings.
- Replace, if a sealed unit.

Chain
- Check for wear and renew if necessary (the latter is very likely). Be prepared to find that the new chain fails to mesh properly with the freewheel sprockets or, if they are badly worn, with the chainwheel teeth. If this is the case, some or all of the transmission will have to be renewed.

- If you are using the rotation method, you will have a fresh chain ready to be refitted at the end of the overhaul.

Rear derailleur
- Check the derailleur pulleys for wear and consider renewing.
- Check that the pivots are working freely and that there is only a little play in them.

Front derailleur
- Check that the pivots are working freely and that there is only a little play in them.

Cables
- Check inner wires for fraying.
- Check casings for kinks.

- Consider renewing inner wires, or the complete wire with casing, if necessary.

Brakes
- Check brake blocks for wear and consider renewing them.
- Regrease pivots.

Screw-on freewheel
- Check action to ensure smooth rotation and play.
- Check sprocket teeth for wear.

Cassette freewheel
- Check freewheel for action and wear.
- Check sprocket teeth for wear.

Wheels
- Remove tires and inner tubes.
- Remove the freewheel and/or sprockets.
- Replace any broken spokes.
- Check spoke tension.
- Check rim for dents or damage.
- Check wheel for trueness.
- Dismantle, clean and regrease bearings.
- Adjust bearings.

Tires and tubes
- Check for splits.
- Check for ozone cracks.
- Check inside for sharp fragments in the carcass.
- Check tubes for rubbing.
- Fit front tire on rear wheel.
- Fit rear tire on front wheel.
- Consider renewing tires and tubes.

Re-assembly checks
- Check rear derailleur throw adjustment.
- Check front derailleur throw adjustment.
- Check and adjust the brake blocks for alignment, binding and toe-in.
- Refit the chain.
- Check for stiff links.
- Check for bent or misaligned teeth.
- Adjust derailleur gear indexing.
- Adjust hub gear selector.
- Check gear function.
- Check front and rear lights.

Nuts and bolts
- Check that all nuts and bolts are tight, using the same list created for the weekly check.

MAINTENANCE TIPS

Bear these tips in mind when undertaking any maintenance or repair task.

Safety

First and foremost, always consider safety when doing any kind of work on your bicycle. Already mentioned is the advisability of wearing safety glasses and chemical-resistant gloves when handling degreaser.

Always keep a simple first aid kit in your workshop. Small cuts and grazes are not that uncommon, and as oil-based lubricants can be quite toxic, any cuts should be cleaned with warm salt water and covered with a bandaid as soon as possible.

Workshop routines

When you have finished working on one component, put away your tools and clear the workspace. Before starting work on another job, make sure you have all the tools and replacement parts necessary, and lay them out in order if you wish.

As you dismantle an assembly, lay the constituent parts out in the order in which you removed them, on a tray. Thus, if you are interrupted, the pieces can be stored away temporarily, without disturbing the order.

You will occasionally need to fit a new bolt which will be too long. It can easily be cut to length with a hacksaw – but this will mutilate the first pitch of the thread. Avoid this problem by screwing a nut onto the bolt before cutting the bolt to length. After cutting, the nut can be unscrewed, thus restoring the leader thread.

When reassembling parts and components on your bicycle, grease all the threads as you put them together – this will make them easier to undo in the future. Another way to prevent nuts and bolts from rusting or becoming stuck is routinely to replace them with a stainless steel equivalent. If you fit stainless Nyloc nuts, the problem of their working loose will be avoided.

Keep your hands as clean as possible

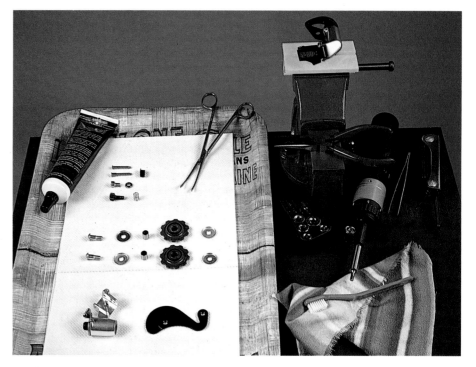

▲ As you dismantle an assembly, lay out the parts in the order in which you take them off. Use a tray so that, if you are interrupted, they can be stored safely without disturbance.

◀ The quickest and simplest way to dress a thread is to place a nut in the vise at an angle. Screw the bolt into it and continue to turn it while you use the file to chamfer the end.

▼ A new bolt has a thread leader (left), but when it is sawn to the required length, the leader becomes mutilated (center). You need to dress the thread to restore it (right).

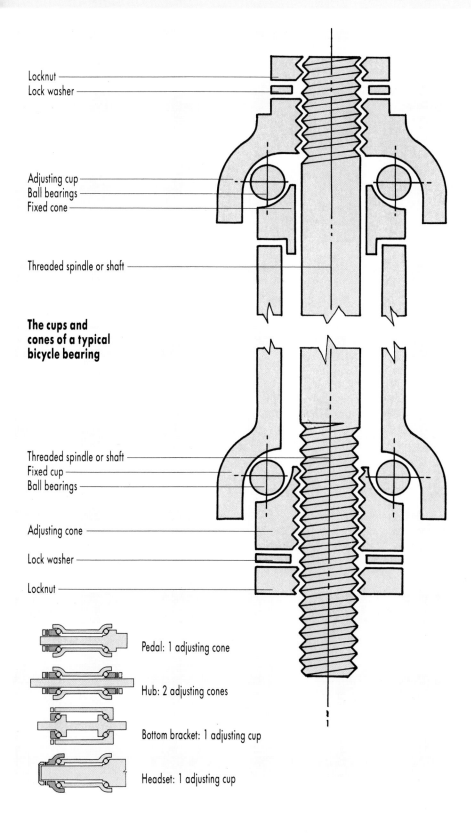

Locknut
Lock washer

Adjusting cup
Ball bearings
Fixed cone

Threaded spindle or shaft

**The cups and
cones of a typical
bicycle bearing**

Threaded spindle or shaft
Fixed cup
Ball bearings

Adjusting cone

Lock washer

Locknut

Pedal: 1 adjusting cone

Hub: 2 adjusting cones

Bottom bracket: 1 adjusting cup

Headset: 1 adjusting cup

when servicing and overhauling a bicycle. This is especially important during reassembly, when grimy hands can easily touch and mark the saddle and handlebar grips. Over the years, I have used numerous hand-cleaners – many of which leave the hands feeling as if they have been stripped of everything bar the final layer of skin. The best cleaning agent that I have found is simple cooking oil, or soya-based body oil. This should be rubbed into your hands and wiped off with an old towel until your hands feel dry. Repeat if necessary. This will leave your hands clean enough to continue working. When all the work on the bicycle has been completed, use the oil as before, and finally wash your hands using a very small amount of liquid soap.

Bearings

The method of adjusting all bearings on the majority of bicycles is broadly similar; the following is intended to give a basic understanding.

Ball bearings run between a cup-shaped and a cone-shaped bearing, known as cups and cones respectively. The whole assembly is referred to as a bearing (or sometimes a ball race) and is mounted on a threaded shaft. The tightness of the bearing is adjusted by turning one of the bearings (either cup or cone, depending on the bearing) against the other on the thread. When the correct tightness is achieved, the whole bearing is locked in position with a locknut, so that it cannot later work loose.

There is usually a minute degree of play in the threads, which means that when the locknut is tightened, it will push the cone or cup slightly further against the ball bearings. For this reason, the bearing should be slightly loose before being finally locked. The exception to this rule is the bottom bracket bearing, where the lockring is tightened against the bottom bracket shell, thus pushing the adjusting cup away from the ball bearings.

FRAME & FORKS

Function

When the frame and front forks are assembled (usually with the headset bearings already in place) the assembly is referred to as a frameset. The frameset is the backbone of your bicycle, and its shape, size and quality determine the comfort and speed of the ride.

Checks

You should make three regular checks on a frameset while the bicycle is fully assembled: first, check that the frame and wheels are aligned. Second, check for bends in the frame tubing. Third, check for cracks at the frame joints.

Alignment can be verified in two ways. The simplest way is to kneel down behind your bicycle while a friend holds it upright. View the front wheel and compare its line with that of the rear wheel; your friend can make slight adjustments to the steering if necessary. If it appears that they will not line up, try the second method. Obtain a piece of string about 13ft long, then follow the method shown in the step-by-step photo sequence.

It is unlikely that a frame with any bent tubes will remain aligned, so misalignment of the wheels often indicates a bent frame – although there's a chance that the wheels have not been fitted to the frame properly, so check this before proceeding. Look for bends in the frame tubes by sighting along their length. Any bend that is not part of the frame's design will be accompanied by rippling and, possibly, by cracking in the paintwork.

If the forks have received an impact from the front, it is possible that damage has been sustained by both the forks and the frame – yet the alignment could appear normal. Look for indications of this damage by sighting down one forkleg; it should not curve toward the frame in relation to the head tube. Check the frame by using your index finger to feel under those

1 With the bicycle in a bicycle stand, tighten the rear brake cable so the rear wheel does not rotate.

frame tubes immediately behind the head tube; look for ripples in the metal and flaking of the paint. If you are involved in a crash, carry out this check as soon as possible afterwards.

After a crash or tumble, it's common to find that the rear derailleur hanger has been bent out of alignment. This should be parallel to (or in the same plane as) the rear wheel. If you suspect that it is misaligned, take it to a good bicycle store where they will check and remedy it with a

▼ Look for any ripples in the metal, or flaking of the paintwork, by feeling with your index finger under those frame tubes immediately behind the head tube. Ripples and flaking indicate damage to the frame from frontal impact.

2 Find the half-way point of the string and wrap it around the back of the rear wheel.

special tool. If it is obviously bent, straighten it carefully with an adjustable wrench as a temporary measure. However, have the bicycle store check it as soon as possible afterwards.

Check the frame all over, particularly at the frame tube joints, for cracks. These will be microscopic in size, but can be highlighted by rubbing the suspect area with chalk and then wiping away the excess. Chalk powder will accumulate in the crack

▼ Cracks in the frame will be microscopically small. Highlight them by rubbing the area with a stick of chalk, then wiping away any excess. Use white chalk for a dark frame and a dark-colored chalk for a light-colored frame.

3 Turn the front wheel so it lines up with the frame. Bring the string forward, either side of the wheel.

4 If the string touches the tires at four points on each side, the wheels are correctly aligned.

and show it up. Use a dark-colored chalk if your frame is light-colored. Have an expert confirm that what you have found is actually a crack in the frame, and not simply a scratch in the paintwork – don't feel stupid if it is only a scratch. Cracks indicate the danger of frame failure, which, if it occurs, could mean that you will end up in the hospital.

The same applies to the brake bosses. Check these for signs of a crack after the calipers have been removed, and the boss cleaned. Brake boss cracks are a rare problem, but the bosses must still be checked regularly, as should all other brazed-on mountings.

Service

There is little you can do to service a frame, other than care for its appearance. All other tasks should be left to a professional.

Touch up any chips in the paintwork by first rubbing the area with emery cloth to give a good key for the paint. If you have to rub down as far as the bare metal, paint that first using metal primer. Allow this to dry before (very gently) rubbing the primer with wet-and-dry paper, to take off any lumps. Then apply two or three coats of matching paint. Do not use cellulose paint or nail varnish because they tend to attack enamel chemically, and most bicycles are finished in enamel.

Overhaul

If you find that your frame is damaged in any way, then any repairs should be carried out by a professional. It is a good idea to consider any improvements that can be made to your frame at the same time, such as an extra set of bottle bosses.

A repaint will probably be necessary once this work has been carried out. Have it done in your favorite color, and it will give both you and your bicycle a new lease of life. The work may take anything from a few days to two or three weeks.

If your frame is in good condition, then at the overhaul stage all you need to do is clean out the steerer and seat tubes.

▼ A derailleur that is out of alignment can be straightened by closing the jaws of an adjustable wrench onto it, then using the handle gently to maneuver it into a better position. Leave the final alignment to a professional.

To clean the inside of the seat and steerer tubes, use a small-diameter rotary wire brush on a flexible drive attached to a power drill. Mount the frame upside down in the vise to prevent grime from running into the bottom bracket. Take care to protect the paintwork with rags or cardboard. Also avoid squeezing the frame tube by doing the vise up too tight. Remember to remove the rag you stuffed inside before you started work.

If you don't have a power drill or flexible drive, you can clean the seat and steerer tubes manually. Tear off a very long strip of rag — ideally this should be about 4in. wide. Soak the strip in degreaser and push it into the seat tube. Next, tear the section of rag you have left hanging out of the tube, and tie the ends to a piece of bar or tube. Turn the bar while slowly withdrawing the strip from the seat tube. Use a similar technique to clean the steerer tube on the front forks.

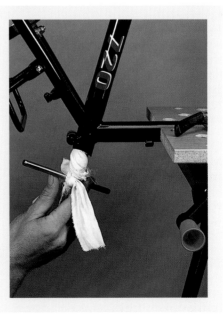

HEADSET

Function
The function of the headset is to allow the steerer tube at the top of the forks to rotate inside the head tube of the frame. The head tube has a bearing at the top and bottom.

Check
There are two problems associated with the headset bearing. The first is simply that it can come loose. Check for looseness by grasping the handlebar with both hands, putting the front (but not the rear) brake on and rocking the bicycle forward and back. Any looseness in the bearing will be obvious by a clicking sound, and by any movement you can see. If the looseness is only slight, confirm it by feeling with your fingertip where the cup and cone meet.

The second problem is caused by your continuing to ride with a loose headset. If you do so, the ball bearings indent the bearing surfaces. Check this by adjusting the headset and rotating it very slowly. If the bearings have been damaged the headset will rotate in a series of pronounced steps. You will require a complete new headset, which should be fitted by a professional.

Service
In the case of the headset, the lower cone is fixed to the fork crown, and the lower cup and upper cone are fixed to the head tube, so the whole assembly is adjusted by the top bearing cup alone. The method is shown in the photo sequence.

Overhaul
Many headsets these days feature small plastic ring seals. These differ in detail from make to make, but all you need to do is carefully note where they are fitted, and which way up they are, before removing them.

Remove the locknut, washer and any spacers or brake cable brackets, then slacken the upper bearing cup about half a turn. Now mount the frame and forks upside down.

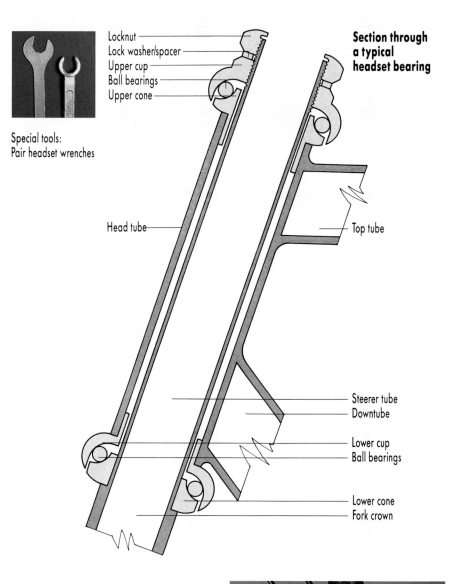

Special tools:
Pair headset wrenches

Locknut
Lock washer/spacer
Upper cup
Ball bearings
Upper cone

Head tube

Section through a typical headset bearing

Top tube

Steerer tube
Downtube

Lower cup
Ball bearings

Lower cone
Fork crown

Unscrew the upper bearing cup with your fingers. Because the frame is upside down, the forks and the lower bearing will remain safely in place while you do this. As you unscrew the upper bearing cup, the ball bearings will stay in the cup. These are usually retained in a circular retainer cage, but look inside the bearing cup

▶ The cone of the lower bearing is fitted to the fork crown, while the cone of the upper bearing and the cup of the lower bearing are fitted to the head tube. You need special tools to remove them, so clean them while they are in place.

36

to see whether they actually are on your model. If they are not, you should hold a container under the end of the steerer to catch them as soon as the bearing cup comes off the end of the steerer tube.

If the ball bearings are in a cage, it is now a simple task to draw the forks out, and to remove the lower retainer cage and put it with the other ball bearings. If the ball bearings are loose, then, while holding the forks in place, remount the frame so that the head tube is horizontal. Hold the container below the lower bearing and withdraw the forks from the head

tube. Catch the ball bearings as the bearing is parted.

Clean the ball bearings in the container. If they are held in retainer cages, you can press them out and put the cages with the other headset components to be cleaned. The ball bearings need not be scrupulously clean – simply clean enough to enable you to count and examine them. The sizes of ball bearing are quite distinct, so simply compare their size with those you have in stock and select the right number of the right size to replace the old ones. If the ball bearings are held in retainer cages, you

can press new ones into the old cage after it has been thoroughly cleaned.

Note that the cone of the upper bearing and the cup of the lower bearing are fitted to the ends of the head tube, and that the cone of the lower bearing is fitted to the fork crown. These three bearings should be cleaned and checked for wear or pitting while they are in place. If they appear to be worn out, you will need to purchase a complete new headset. The old fixed cups and cones should be removed, and new ones fitted. This job requires special tools, so leave it to a professional.

To reassemble the headset, mount the frame upside down, as before. Smear some grease around the inside of the lower cup (which is uppermost in this position). Using either tweezers or your fingers, put loose ball bearings around the inside of the cup. If, for some reason, you do not know how many have come out, put in as many as you can, but leave a space for one more. If the ball bearings are in a cage, simply place a retained set into the cup and cover with a little more grease. If there is a ring seal, place it in position and make sure you have placed the retainer cage the correct way up. If not, the headset will not adjust properly.

Carefully lower the fork steerer tube into the head tube. Smear grease around the inside of the upper bearing cup and place ball bearings around it. Place the ring seal in position. Spread some grease on the threads of the steerer tube and screw the upper bearing cup onto it until it is hand-tight against the ball bearings.

The frame should now be remounted upright. Place the tanged washer over the top of the steerer tube, ensuring that the tang engages with the groove in the thread if there is one. There are also flatted and round headset washers and forks. Place any other spacers or cable stop brackets over the top of the steerer, followed by the locknut. The headset can now be adjusted and locked.

1 Slacken the headset locknut just enough to release the upper bearing cup.

2 Tighten down the upper bearing cup until no looseness is felt in the assembly.

3 Tighten the locknut down onto the upper bearing cup and hold it securely in position.

4 Unscrew the upper bearing cup until it is tight against the headset locknut.

HANDLEBAR & STEM

Function

The handlebars enable you to steer your bicycle, while having the control levers within easy reach. A well-designed handlebar assembly will enable you to steer while operating the control levers with maximum comfort, safety and convenience.

Check

First check that your handlebar is indeed comfortable when you ride, and that the brake and gear levers are within reach and operate satisfactorily (I assume that your brakes and gears are already adjusted and working properly). The handlebar can be angled, and the control levers positioned, to suit you. To adjust the handlebar position further, the stem can be moved up or down in the frame. If you are moving the handlebars up, make sure that the minimum insertion mark is not visible. If the front brake cable stop is part of the stem, you may have to disconnect the cable from the brake. Otherwise, release the straddle wire and readjust the brake afterwards.

When you have the handlebar stem at a height that suits you, mark it with masking tape before you remove it again. Even if you do not want to alter the height of the stem,

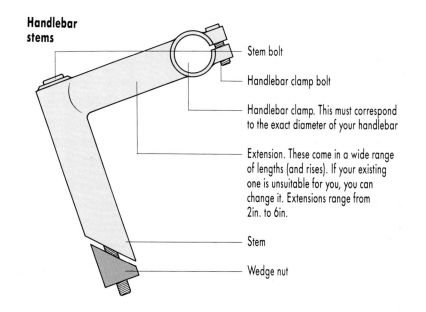

Handlebar stems

Stem bolt

Handlebar clamp bolt

Handlebar clamp. This must correspond to the exact diameter of your handlebar

Extension. These come in a wide range of lengths (and rises). If your existing one is unsuitable for you, you can change it. Extensions range from 2in. to 6in.

Stem

Wedge nut

you should check that the handlebar is set at a right angle to the line of the front wheel and rotate it accordingly. All these adjustments use the technique shown for removal of the handlebar assembly.

Handlebars can break, and not always through simple brute force. The clamps that hold the handlebar in the stem, and those of the control levers, can sometimes produce stress risers if the edge of the clamp is sharp.

Clamps can also cause scratching when control levers are being fitted to the handlebar, especially if both are made of aluminum.

If your hand grips are not secure, clean the insides of them, and the handlebar ends too, using lighter fluid. Refit them (using lighter fluid as a lubricant), then leave the grips for several hours to allow the fluid to evaporate. If this doesn't work, refit the grips using WD40 instead, again

1 Mark the height of your stem with a piece of masking tape where the stem enters the frame. Loosen or disconnect the front brake if necessary.

2 Slacken the stem bolt, which is positioned at the top of the stem, by one or two turns. This is usually a 6mm Allen socket.

3 Using a rubber hammer (or a metal hammer with a hardwood drift to soften the blow), give the stem bolt a sharp blow.

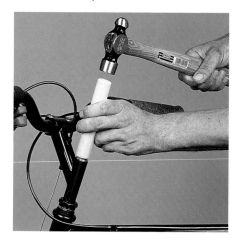

Handlebar grips are often difficult to remove. Carefully slide a slim screwdriver along the inside of the grip – with the blade flat against the handlebar to avoid scratching. This will enable you to lift the open end of the grip and to spray some thin lubricant inside. Remove the screwdriver and twist the grip to spread the lubricant. It should now be possible to wind it off slowly. If this does not work immediately, you may have to repeat the operation to allow the lube to penetrate further inside the grip. Be sure to clean the handlebar, and inside the grip, of all traces of grease before finally refitting.

▲ If you find a deep scratch, it can be filed carefully until it is no more than a smooth depression. This may be enough to prevent the scratch from developing into a dangerous crack later on.

leaving them for a period of time for the lubricant to dry. If that does not work, you will have to resort to using contact cement. If you do this, you will not be able to remove the grips again except by cutting them, after which you will not, of course, be able to use them again.

Removal

The same technique is used to remove the handlebar assembly and to adjust the position of the stem. Follow the method shown in the step-by-step photo sequence.

Overhaul

Your handlebar assembly should be mounted in the bench vise with the handlebar stem set horizontally. First remove one or both hand grips, or the handlebar tape, if fitted.

Once the grips have been removed, the clamps of the control levers can be slackened and the levers removed. Next, slacken the stem clamp and withdraw the handlebar. Be careful to avoid scratching the handlebar when doing this.

If you discover a crack in the handlebar, or stem, then you must replace it. If you find a deep scratch, this can be filed carefully until it is simply a smooth depression: this may be sufficient to prevent it from developing into a crack. However, you must remember to give the area special attention at all subsequent weekly checks.

Feel inside the lever and stem clamps for any scratches or burrs and, with the aid of a lamp, file these as smooth as you can. At the same time you may consider filing a slight chamfer onto the edges of the clamps if they are sharp.

4 The wedge-nut on the other end of the stem bolt, which normally holds the stem tight inside the steerer tube, should now have been released.

5 If the stem cannot be moved, spray some penetrating lubricant at the point where the stem enters the frame and leave it for a short time.

6 Remove the stem by turning and pulling it upwards, while keeping the forks steady by holding the front wheel between your legs.

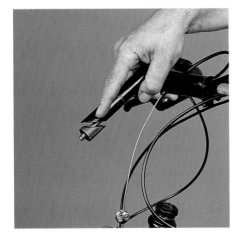

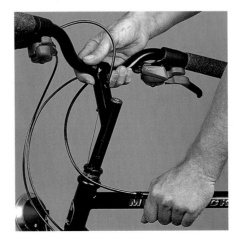

SADDLE & SEAT POST

Function

Basically, your saddle should provide you with a comfortable place to sit and pedal. The seat post allows the saddle to be used at different heights. In addition, the clamp built into the top of the seat post is used to adjust the front and back positioning of the saddle as well as its angle to the top tube and the ground.

Check

The saddle should be stable, and should not rotate or tilt while you ride. There should be no irregular lumps or splits in the material of the saddle top, and (if it is a leather saddle) it should be stretched quite tight.

To be practical, the time to check the comfort of your saddle is while you are riding along. Bear in mind that the adjustment of the saddle position is as critical to comfort as the saddle itself. As a starting point to finding the saddle position that suits you, position it according to the accepted formula by following this procedure.

First, take your inside leg measurement from crotch bone to the floor, with no shoes on. Next, multiply this figure by a factor of 1.09 to calculate the correct distance from pedal to saddle.

Align the cranks with the seat tube and loosen the clamp on the seat post. Move the saddle up or down until the top of the saddle is the required distance from the top of the pedal which is farthest from the saddle, and tighten the seat post clamp firmly. Now loosen the saddle clamp and adjust the tilt of the saddle until the top is horizontal, and tighten the clamp again.

With the bicycle supported vertically, sit on the saddle and turn the cranks until they are horizontal. Using a piece of string with a weight at the lower end, check that the center of the forward knee is vertically above the pedal axis.

Dismount and loosen the saddle clamp again. Move the saddle for-

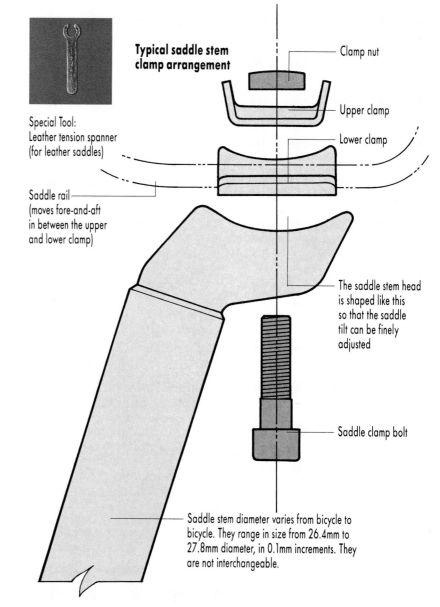

Special Tool:
Leather tension spanner (for leather saddles)

Typical saddle stem clamp arrangement

Clamp nut

Upper clamp

Lower clamp

Saddle rail (moves fore-and-aft in between the upper and lower clamp)

The saddle stem head is shaped like this so that the saddle tilt can be finely adjusted

Saddle clamp bolt

Saddle stem diameter varies from bicycle to bicycle. They range in size from 26.4mm to 27.8mm diameter, in 0.1mm increments. They are not interchangeable.

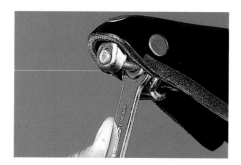

◄ Some leather saddles need to be tensioned from time to time. Use a special wrench to work the tension adjuster found under the nose of the saddle.

► Tightening the saddle clamp sometimes requires more force than it is possible to apply with a normal Allen wrench. Extend the arm of the Allen wrench when you have completed any adjustment by putting a tube over it. This will provide extra leverage. However, be careful to avoid shearing the bolt.

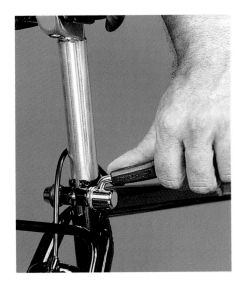

1 Undo the clamp, or open the quick release, on the frame at the bottom of the seat post.

2 Withdraw the saddle and seat post together by twisting while pulling them out of the frame.

3 Loosen the clamp at the top of the seat post to remove the saddle.

4 When the clamp is loose enough, turn the top part around to release the saddle rails.

ward or backward as required. Tighten the clamp and try the position again.

If you find that you want the saddle to be higher in the frame, check that the seat post is not extended beyond its minimum insertion mark. A new seat post will have to be bought if it is, and it is vital that the new one is of the correct diameter for your frame. It may be stamped next to the minimum insertion mark.

Service
If the seat post rotates in the frame, even when the quick release is closed, then try adjusting the quick release to make it tighter. If this has no effect, it is probable that the seat post is not of the correct diameter for the seat tube, into which the seat post fits. You must buy a new one.

If the saddle tilts while you're riding along, the saddle clamp at the top of the stem should be tightened.

If the saddle top is made of stretch fabric, any splits can be sewn together. If the saddle is made of vinyl, then a temporary repair can be made using a special vinyl glue. Splits in a leather saddle cannot be mended.

Removal
Follow the method shown in the step-by-step photo sequence.

Overhaul
At the overhaul stage, if your saddle and seat post are in good order, there are only a few tasks to complete. The saddle should be removed from the seat post, and all the components cleaned up. If you have a leather saddle, it should be treated with leather dressing or saddle soap after any slack in the material has been taken up. (If your leather saddle is the type that has support springs under the top, there will be no need to tension the leather.) With a sprung saddle, place a drop of oil on each pivot, and on the ends of the springs supporting the top to prevent the saddle from creaking as you ride.

PEDALS

Function

Pedals allow you to rotate the cranks with your feet; they should be comfortable, should grip your feet easily, and should rotate freely at right-angles to the crank.

Check

To check the pedal bearings for looseness, rock them while holding the crank firmly. If they are loose you will feel a slight clicking. Check for tightness by turning the pedal very slowly, listening for any grinding sound from the bearings.

Service

Few of the cheaper makes of pedal are easy to service. The dust cap is often fitted flush, and the pedal cage covers the dust cap, making access to the bearings impracticable. When the bearings are worn to an unacceptable degree, these cheaper makes have to be thrown away.

Pedals of a better quality or design can be adjusted more easily. To adjust the tightness of the bearings you must first remove the dust cap on the outer end of the spindle. This may unscrew, sometimes requiring a special tool particular to that model or make (ask at your local bicycle store). If a dust cap does not unscrew, then you simply prise it off, using a small screwdriver under the edge.

Inside the pedal body you will find the locknut, and if you look beyond that you will see the lockwasher and the adjusting cone, which has a slot on each side.

This is one of the more difficult adjustments to make on your bicycle. The best way to tackle it is to unscrew the locknut a few turns. Using a small screwdriver again,

Special tool:
Extra-long pedal wrench

Section through a typical pedal

Steel spindle threaded for crank

Fixed cone machined onto the spindle

Weather seal

Ball bearings

Steel fixed cup
(press-fit into alloy
pedal body)

Alloy pedal body

Steel fixed cup
Ball bearings
Adjusting cone
Lock washer
Locknut
Dust cap

▼ To prevent the ball bearings falling out, take the pedal spindle in your index finger and thumb by the threads at the adjusting end and allow the pedal to hang from your fingers.

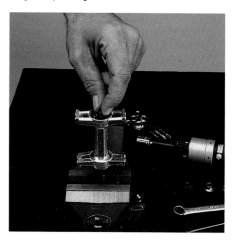

▼ Note that the left-side pedal has a left-handed thread. Unscrew it from the crank in a clockwise fashion. The right-hand pedal unscrews in the normal (that is, counterclockwise) way.

1 Rotate the crank to a forward position so that it points up at about 45°, and place the wrench across the flats on the spindle. Use the longest wrench you have.

2 Keeping the crank in position, push the wrench down until the pedal begins to unscrew. If the pedal does not give, either extend the wrench with a tube, or use your foot.

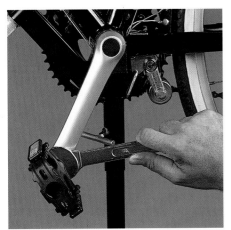

3 Rotate the crank forward while holding the wrench at the same angle, in the manner of a connecting rod on a steam engine's driving wheel. This is the correct rotation for removal.

4 To refit or tighten a pedal, use this method in reverse. Rotating the cranks backward while holding the pedal spindle with the wrench does not require the chain to be removed.

nudge the lockwasher to loosen it and then insert the blade of the screwdriver into one of the slots on the cone. Turn the cone clockwise until it is tight against the ball bearings, then back it off an eighth of a turn. Now tighten the locknut down again, and check that the adjustment is neither too tight nor too loose. If it is either of these, you will have to re-adjust it. Once the pedal is turning nicely, refit the dustcap.

Removal

If you follow the method shown in the step-by-step photo sequence, you will always get it right.

Overhaul

Mount a pedal in the vise jaws so that the jaws close on the flats at the threaded end of the spindle, with the pedal vertical. Remove the dustcap. Unscrew the locknut and remove it, along with the lockwasher. The

adjusting cone can then be unscrewed with a small screwdriver or a pin wrench. Put these items into a tray of degreaser to soak. While the pedal is in the vise, the ball bearings cannot fall out. Either pick them out with a pair of tweezers or carefully undo the vise while holding the upper end of the spindle and the body together in your hand. Turn the pedal over to let the ball bearings fall out into a container held ready for that purpose.

Keeping the spindle horizontal, carefully withdraw it from the pedal body, holding it over a container to catch the ball bearings when the bearing comes apart. Keep all the ball bearings in the container so you can count them, and check their size against the new ones. Put the spindle into the tray of degreaser with the other parts for cleaning.

Now clean the bearing cups, which are press-fitted into the pedal body, by flushing through with degreaser. Check these bearing cups, once they are clean, for pitting or wear. You may have to buy a new pair of pedals if they are badly damaged by wear.

To prepare for reassembly, open the vise just wide enough to accept the flats on the spindle. Smear grease into the crank-end bearing cup (inside the body of the pedal) and then place the correct number of ball bearings around the inside. The grease will hold them in place, and you should leave enough space for one more ball bearing to go in. Hold the pedal so that the newly fitted bearings are at the top, then carefully introduce the threaded end of the spindle into the central tube of the pedal body. Take the spindle by the threads at the adjusting end, and allow the pedal to hang from your fingers. Set the spindle into the vise. You can now grease the inside of the opposite bearing cup and put the remaining ball bearings around the inside. Fit the adjusting cone and tanged lockwasher, then screw the locknut down and adjust as above.

CRANKSET & BOTTOM BRACKET

Function
The crankset is comprised of two cranks, with the right-hand crank carrying the chain on the chainrings. The crankset turns on the bottom bracket bearings.

Check
Check for any looseness of the bottom bracket bearings by rotating the left-hand crank until it is next to the chainstay. Hold both cranks and try to move them in and out against the chainstay. If movement is felt in both cranks at once, the bottom bracket bearing will need adjusting. (If the movement is felt in one crank only, it has worked loose on the bottom bracket spindle, and should be tightened.) To check for tightness of the bottom bracket bearings, turn the cranks very slowly and listen for a grating sound.

Check the straightness of both cranks: they should rotate so that the pedal is parallel to the bottom bracket.

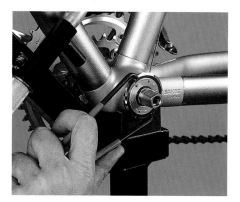

1 Hook a C wrench onto the lockring and unscrew it about half a turn.

Bent cranks can sometimes be straightened, but you will probably have to buy a new set.

Chainrings should be checked with the chain removed. First spin the crankset around to check for buckles; then turn it slowly to allow a detailed inspection, during which you should look for tooth wear caused by the chain. If the gap between the teeth is visibly deeper than usual, you have a problem. (Very badly worn teeth develop a hooked shape.) A worn chainring must be renewed. Look also for bent teeth on the chainrings.

Service
Today, sealed unit bearings are often fitted. These cannot be serviced and must be replaced when worn out.

Special tools:
Crank extractor tool
Crank bolt wrench
C wrench
Pin wrench

Section through a typical bottom bracket bearing

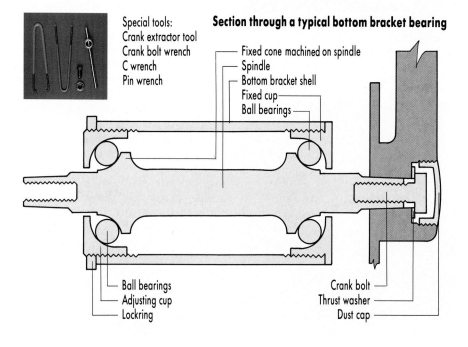

Fixed cone machined on spindle
Spindle
Bottom bracket shell
Fixed cup
Ball bearings

Ball bearings
Adjusting cup
Lockring

Crank bolt
Thrust washer
Dust cap

1 Remove the dustcap with the appropriate tool, depending on the make of crank.

2 With a socket wrench, remove the crank retaining bolt and washer.

3 Screw the outer collar of the extractor tool into the aperture on the crank.

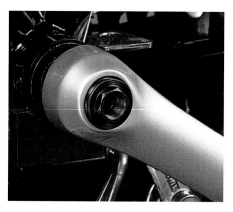

2 Using a pin wrench, tighten the adjusting cup to remove any play in the bearing.

3 While holding the adjusting cup in place, tighten the lockring firmly.

4 It is often possible to carry out this adjustment without removing the crank.

In a bottom bracket bearing, the fixed cup is on the right-hand side and the adjusting cup is on the other end. To adjust the bearing, follow the method shown in the step-by-step photo sequence.

A buckled chainwheel can be straightened in a crude way by finding the point of maximum deflection and then striking it firmly with a rubber hammer and a hardwood drift. A misaligned tooth can be straightened by closing the jaws of an adjustable wrench over the tooth and gently levering the tooth back into alignment with the other teeth.

Crank removal
Follow the method shown in the step-by-step photo sequence.

Overhaul: Bottom bracket
Use a C wrench to unscrew the lockring, and a pin wrench to remove the adjusting cup bearing. Catch the ball bearings (if they are loose) in a container held underneath. While holding the spindle in place with your finger and thumb, lay the frame on its right-hand side. Now withdraw the spindle; the remaining ball bearings will fall out through the hole in the fixed cup.

If you own a fixed cup wrench, which is a specialist tool, the fixed cup can be unscrewed in a clockwise direction. Otherwise clean it in place.

After cleaning all the parts, smear some grease into the fixed cup and place the ball bearings around the inside of the cup. If you have

removed it, screw the fixed cup back into the bottom bracket shell. Insert the longer end of the spindle through the fixed cup. Smear the adjusting cup with grease, put the remaining ball bearings around the inside and carefully put the adjusting cup over the end of the spindle. Screw it into the bottom bracket shell along with the lockring and, using a C wrench and a pin wrench, adjust it following the method shown in the photo sequence.

Examine the inside of the square aperture in the crank with a lamp. If there are any burrs, gently file them away. Remove the crank retaining bolt and press the crank onto the square sectioned ends of the spindle. Replace the retaining bolt and tighten.

4 Screw in the extractor bolt, and continue until the crank is released from the spindle.

5 Refit the crank retaining bolt and washer in the spindle so that you don't lose them.

6 To tighten a crank, tighten the crank retaining bolt firmly, then replace the dustcap.

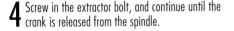

CHAIN

Function

A roller chain is the most efficient means of transmitting the rotary motion of the chainwheel to the rear sprocket – and thus to the ground, via the rear wheel. Of all the assemblies on a bicycle, the chain requires the most attention.

Check

During good weather, you only have to check that your chain is not dry; if it is, simply use a spray lube on it. Point the spray, from a forward position, at the upper jockey pulley, spraying while you turn the pedals backward. This serves to place the lube onto the inner surface of the chain: the centrifugal effect of the rotating chain will then force the lube through the links of the chain before throwing off any surplus. Take great care to avoid getting lube onto the braking surface of the rims while you are spraying the chain.

After it has been removed from the bicycle, the chain should be checked against a ruler for wear. It should also be checked for stiff or twisted links once it has been refitted.

Removal

If your chain has become really grimy, it is a good idea to give it a cursory cleaning before removing and handling it. To do this, hold a

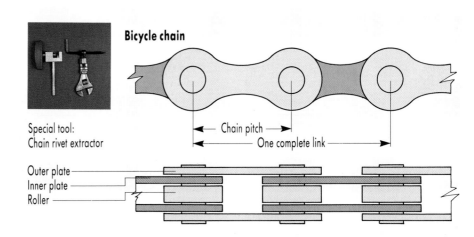

Bicycle chain

Special tool:
Chain rivet extractor

Chain pitch

One complete link

Outer plate
Inner plate
Roller

rag (preferably made of terrycloth) around the lower run of the chain while turning the pedals backward. This will get the worst of the grime off. Alternatively, you may prefer to use a purpose-made chain bath.

With a derailleur gear system, the chain has to be broken by partly removing one of the rivets that hold it together. When doing this, it is important to ensure that the chain is not under tension. You can usually minimize tension by setting the chain onto the smallest chainring and the smallest sprocket. If this doesn't provide enough slack, you can slip the chain off the chainring so that it runs on the bottom bracket shell. The best way, however, is to design an S hook

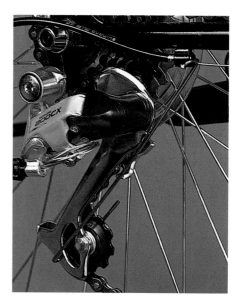

▲ The best way to relieve tension in a chain so that you can break it more easily is to design an S hook, using an old spoke. One end of the S goes around the pulley cage; now, pulling it forward, hook the other end around the cable stop on the chainstay. Keep the hook specially for this job in the future.

◀ A chain bath hooks onto the pulley cage and opens up to allow you to insert the chain. When closed, the chain is pulled through rotating brushes in a bath of degreaser when the pedals are turned backward. Afterwards, fill the chain bath with water and rinse both the bath and the chain in the same manner. The manufacturers claim that you can both clean and lube the chain using this device, but it does not remove all the dirt and grime that sticks to the teeth of the chainwheels and sprockets.

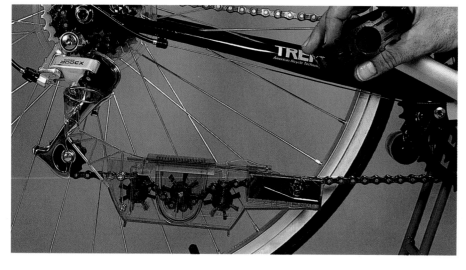

1 Place the chain tool on the chain and align the rivet pusher with the rivet head.

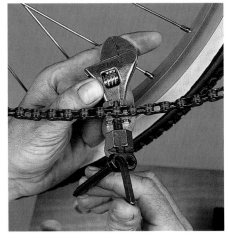

2 Push the rivet out by turning the threaded shaft eleven half-turns with the handle.

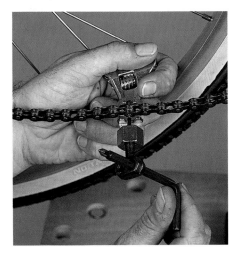

3 Unscrew the shaft until the pusher is clear of the chain, then remove the tool.

4 Hold the chain on either side of the rivet, then gently flex it and snap the chain apart.

from an old spoke, which can be used to pull the jockey cage forward.

Remember that the intention is to push the rivet out just far enough to enable you to snap the links apart, then back together again. This will make it easier to rejoin the chain when refitting. Follow the method shown in the step-by-step photo sequence.

Cleaning

Really effective and thorough cleaning is vital if the bicycle chain is to last a long time. Cleaning can be a tedious process, but it will save you a lot of money in the long run.

Place the dirty chain in a metal tray of degreaser and slosh it about, using a stiff toothbrush to get rid of any stubborn grime. Be careful to avoid splashing the degreaser around too much if you are doing this in the kitchen sink, and be sure to wear chemical-resistant gloves, especially if you suffer from any skin condition.

Next, remove the chain from the tray and lay it on some old newspaper. Dab it as clean and dry as possible, using an old rag. Pour the degreaser you have just used from the tray into the recycling bottle to allow the solids to settle. Clean the tray with water and a little detergent, then dry it thoroughly. Put the chain back into the tray and pour on some fresh, clean degreaser. Give the chain a second clean, using the technique described above. This second wash will probably be sufficient, but give

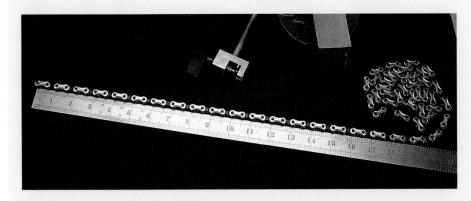

It is easy to measure how badly your chain has worn by placing it alongside a tape measure. Pull the links apart so the chain is as long as possible. Measure as many links as possible. Set the center of the first rivet on zero, then count out the maximum number of links. The chain is badly worn and must be discarded if:

- 5 links measure 5$\frac{1}{32}$in.
- 10 links measure 10$\frac{1}{16}$in.
- 20 links measure 20$\frac{1}{8}$ in.
- 30 links measure 30$\frac{3}{16}$in.

CHAIN

it a third wash to be absolutely sure.

After the final wash, simply pour off the used degreaser for recycling and wash the chain in the same tray, using hot soapy water. Give the chain a vigorous shake in the soapy water, and then rinse it several times in clean water. Both the chain and tray should now be perfectly clean.

The chain should now be dried in the tray, and the best way I have found is to put both chain and tray in an oven at about 212°F (100°C) for 30 minutes or so. Exercise extreme caution when using this method: never leave the oven unattended; make sure that you have a fire extinguisher on hand in case of an accident; and remember to wear a sturdy pair of fire-proof, insulated gloves when removing the tray from the oven.

The chain is now ready for soaking in petroleum oil, if that is the lubrication you choose to use. Alternatively, if you prefer to use a synthetic lubricant, allow the chain to cool before lubing it. Refer to pages 20-21 for some tips on lubricants.

Oil-based lubrication
Some cyclists prefer to lubricate their chain using a commercial wax which contains graphite. This comes supplied in a shallow pan, which is designed to be placed on a stove at a very low setting until the wax becomes liquid. At this point, using an S hook to handle it, lower the chain into the liquid and allow it to 'cook' for a short while. (Be sure to follow the manufacturer's instructions carefully throughout the process. Never leave the pan unattended while the wax is liquid, or while the stove is on, under any circumstances.)

Now, carefully remove the chain with the S hook, remembering that it will drip liquid wax, and hang it up, with a metal tray beneath to catch any drips. Wipe off all the surplus while the wax is still in a fluid state. Finally leave the chain to cool down, allowing the wax to solidify within the rollers of the chain.

Some experienced cyclists prefer to use transmission oil of the 'hypoid' grade to lube their chains. This grade of oil ranges in viscosity from SAE80 to SAE120, and is available in gallon cans. The technique here is to place the can of oil on the floor below a hook which is positioned high enough for the chain to hang from, allowing the lowest link to dangle in the top of the can. Warm the chain in the oven (ensure that it is not so

1 Set the rear derailleur to align with the smallest sprocket, and the front derailleur to align with the smallest chainring.

5 Bring the two ends of the chain together and snap the links into place. Relieve any tension in the chain if necessary.

hot that it causes the oil to burn), then use the S hook to lower the chain very carefully right into the oil, leaving the S hook over the lip of the can. This sticky oil penetrates the links and bearings of the chain more effectively when the chain is warm.

After about 15 minutes, slowly lift the chain out of the can and hang it on the hook, making sure that the last link remains just inside the can. Allow any surplus oil to drain back into the can. When the chain has cooled, wipe it with a clean rag, starting at the top and drawing the cloth down so that the oil drips back into

A 3-chain rotation system:

	Week 1	Week 2	Week 3	Week 4	Week 5
Chain 1	In use	Cleaning	Lubed	In use	Cleaning
Chain 2	Cleaning	Lubed	In use	Cleaning	Lubed
Chain 3	Lubed	In use	Cleaning	Lubed	In use

A 5-chain rotation system:

	Week 1	Week 2	Week 3	Week 4	Week 5
Chain 1	In use	Soaking	Cleaning	Lubed	Lubed
Chain 2	Soaking	Cleaning	Lubed	Lubed	In use
Chain 3	Cleaning	Lubed	Lubed	In use	Soaking
Chain 4	Lubed	Lubed	In use	Soaking	Cleaning
Chain 5	Lubed	In use	Soaking	Cleaning	Lubed

A 5-chain rotation system is more flexible; you could choose to have one cleaning and lubing session every five weeks. However, use chains in strict rotation to avoid unequal wear.

2 Feed the chain over the smallest sprocket, around the front of the jockey pulley, behind the idler pulley, and pull some links through.

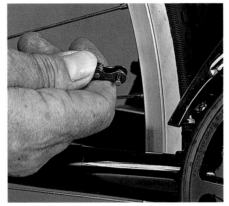

3 Make sure that the displaced rivet is at the other end of the chain and that it will protrude outward, away from the bicycle.

4 Feed the other end of the chain through the front derailleur cage, over the smallest chainring, and pull it through.

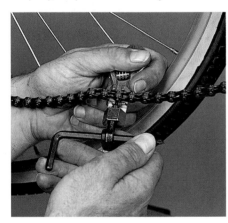

6 Use the chain tool to push the rivet back into place by aligning the pusher with the rivet and turning it eleven half-turns.

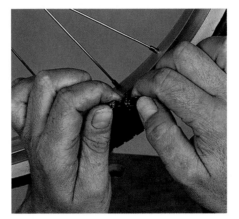

7 Hold the chain on either side of the link and gently flex it laterally. This will spread the link apart so that it is not stiff.

8 Now turn the pedals backward and watch the link. If it doesn't run smoothly, it may still be stiff, so flex it again.

the can. The chain is now ready to use. It should be wiped dry again after the first ride. Although the chain is well-lubed internally, the oil will attract dust, which will mean that the chain will have become quite grimy when it is time to remove it again for the next service.

Synthetic-based lubrication
For synthetic lubrication, the chain should be allowed to cool, and then laid on a flat surface with the plates vertical and the rivets horizontal. Synthetic chain lube is very thin and inherently penetrative. Apply it

by putting two or three drops onto each link of the chain. Alternatively, refit the chain dry, and lube the chain with a spray, as described above. Synthetic chain lube evaporates dry and does not attract dust as do oil-based lubricants.

Chain rotation system
If you continue to use the same chain until it is worn out, when you eventually fit a new one, there is a good chance that it will not mesh with the teeth of the sprockets or, less likely, of the chainrings. This will be because the old chain will have worn into the

teeth, which will, in turn, have worn down to suit the old chain. The only remedy is to buy a completely new set of sprockets and perhaps chainrings, which will cost at least ten times as much as a new chain.

To avoid this problem, operate a chain rotation system, using as many chains as you like. The idea is that although each chain wears into the teeth at the same rate, yet each one has a full wear life. The life of your chainwheels and sprockets is thus extended according to the number of chains you choose to run in your rotation system.

DERAILLEURS

Function

Derailleur gear systems allow the rider to change the ratio between the rate at which he pedals and the speed at which he travels by shifting the chain from one sprocket, or chainwheel, to another. The rear derailleur shifts the chain at the rear and is controlled by the right-hand gear-shift lever on the handlebar or frame. A similar front derailleur is controlled by the left-hand lever.

In the last few years, derailleur systems have improved and each manufacturer has introduced different innovations to optimize performance and efficiency. The advice given here is general, but it will provide you with the basic information: you can then adapt it so it applies to your particular system. However, it is very much worth getting hold of the manufacturer's specific instructions for your particular derailleur.

Check

Most present-day derailleur systems are indexed to allow 'positive' ratio changes. This means that different ratios are selected by moving the gear shift lever one click. The old friction-type derailleur required the rider to select a ratio without the benefit of any positive click, but simply by feel. Unlike friction systems, though, the modern indexed systems can easily go out of adjustment with time and use. You will probably become aware of this poor adjustment while riding: gear changes become difficult (with the chain slipping). Or, in one gear or another, you may hear a clattering noise, although otherwise the transmission will be functioning properly.

If you find that the chain sometimes overrides, becoming jammed at the rear either between the sprocket cluster and the spokes, or between the cluster and the drop-out, or is thrown off the chainrings at the front, the throw-limiter should be adjusted to prevent this.

The rear derailleur pulleys are renewed at each overhaul, but they should also be checked regularly for wear. Using your finger and thumb, grip each pulley and feel for worn bearings. Note that the jockey pulley on most indexed rear derailleurs has a built-in lateral play. Worn pulley wheels can affect gear efficiency.

A final check, especially after a crash, is for any misalignment of the rear derailleur or, more usually, of the pulley cage (the front derailleur is very rarely damaged in accidents). It is really best to buy a new one, but it is always worth trying to straighten the old one first. Before attempting this, make sure that the hanger on the frame is properly aligned. See pages 34 and 35 for more information about this particular problem.

Service

Adjusting the gears is one of the final tasks, and should be carried out once you have refitted the chain but before you go for a test ride.

▲ Both the front and rear derailleurs have a throw adjustment which governs their side-to-side movement. Each is usually marked with an H or an L, denoting either the High-end or Low-end of the travel that that particular screw affects.

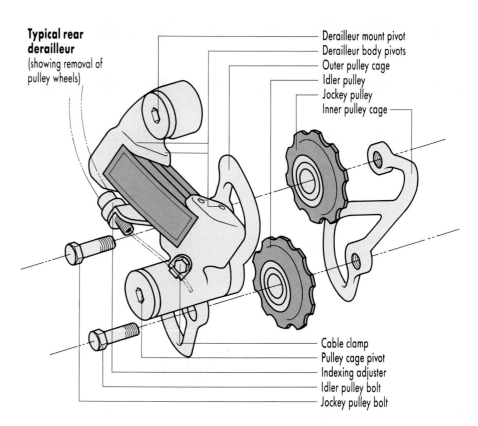

Typical rear derailleur
(showing removal of pulley wheels)

Derailleur mount pivot
Derailleur body pivots
Outer pulley cage
Idler pulley
Jockey pulley
Inner pulley cage

Cable clamp
Pulley cage pivot
Indexing adjuster
Idler pulley bolt
Jockey pulley bolt

▲ Misalignment of the rear derailleur or of the pulley cage should be checked if either receives any impact. You can try to straighten them, but first make sure that the hanger on the frame is properly aligned.

▼ The pulley wheels should frequently be checked for wear by gripping the outside edge with the finger and thumb. If there is noticeable bearing wear, they should be renewed.

Both the front and rear derailleurs have a throw-limiting adjustment which controls the side-to-side movement of the chain cage. If the chain tends to jump off when you change gear, the throw must be checked. On each mechanism you will find a pair of small screw heads, each usually marked with either an H or an L. The letters denote the High-end and Low-end respectively of the travel that the screw affects.

To adjust the throw limit correctly you must, first, shift the rear derailleur so that the chain moves onto the smallest sprocket. Second, you must shift the front derailleur so that the chain moves onto the largest chainring. Now, return to the rear derailleur and check by eye that the smallest sprocket is aligned with both pulley wheels. If they do not align, tighten or loosen the throw adjuster marked H on the rear derailleur until they do align. Check alignment by

▼ You can replace your lower idler pulley with the standard type (on the left), which has a small metal bush and a grease shroud on each side of the wheel. Alternatively, you may choose to upgrade by installing a sealed bearing idler pulley.

turning the pedals. Now turn your attention to the front derailleur. The outer cage plate should be close to the chain, but not touching it. If it is rubbing, or is further out, tighten or loosen the throw adjuster marked H until it is just right.

Now shift the chain onto the largest sprocket and the smallest chainring. Check that the largest sprocket and the two pulley wheels are aligned. If they are not, tighten or loosen the adjuster marked L on the rear derailleur until they do so. On the front derailleur, the inside chain cage plate should be no more than $\frac{1}{16}$in. or so from the chain. Tighten or loosen the throw adjuster marked L until the chain cage is correctly positioned.

Accurate indexing adjustment should only be carried out once the throw adjustment has been completed. This is a matter of making very small, careful control cable adjustments to both the front and rear derailleurs.

Rear derailleur indexing adjustment is carried out by turning an adjuster where the control cable enters the mechanism at the rear. This

DERAILLEURS

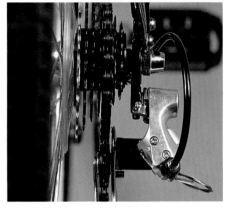

1 With the bicycle held in a stand, rotate the crank and, by operating the control levers, shift the chain onto the largest chainring and the second-from-smallest sprocket.

2 Check by eye that the sprocket and both pulley wheels are aligned. If they are not, bring them into alignment by tightening or slackening the cable adjuster at the rear of the derailleur.

3 Rotate the crank again and shift the chain onto the next largest sprocket by working the control lever. Look again to see if the sprocket and pulley wheels are aligned.

adjuster determines the exact measurement of each shift of the rear derailleur, which must be the same as the gap between each of the freewheel sprockets. Follow the method shown in the photo sequence above.

The front derailleur indexing adjustment is less complicated to carry out: shift the chain onto the middle chainring on a triple or the inner on a double, and onto the

fourth sprocket of the cluster at the rear. Adjust the control cable tension with the adjuster on the shift lever so that the chain runs centrally within the cage. It should be noted that, when the chain is shifted across more than four sprockets, the front derailleur will need to be moved a half-step, because the chain line will have moved sufficiently to cause it to rub on the chain cage.

Overhaul: Rear derailleur
Lay the derailleur on a work surface. Remove each pulley wheel by unscrewing the pulley bolts. This will also remove the inner pulley cage. Note the order in which you remove the wheels and shims, and compare these with the new ones, which should be kept close on hand.

The whole derailleur can now be cleaned in degreaser with the paint-

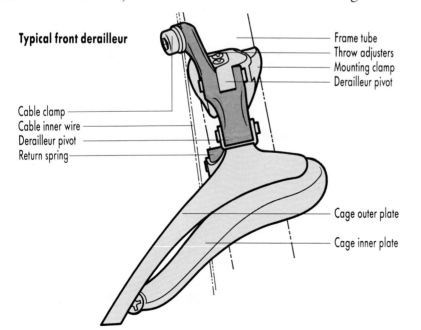

Typical front derailleur

- Frame tube
- Throw adjusters
- Mounting clamp
- Derailleur pivot
- Cable clamp
- Cable inner wire
- Derailleur pivot
- Return spring
- Cage outer plate
- Cage inner plate

1 With the clamp lightly tightened, use your fingers to push the derailleur to its outermost position, against the effect of the return spring.

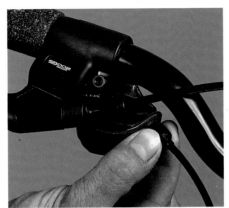

4 Tighten or loosen the adjuster as necessary to align them. The shifting dimension is now set and, since the increments are all the same, shifts will work across the whole cluster.

5 Now the cable tension should be adjusted using the adjuster on the shift lever. Rotate the transmission and shift the chain onto each sprocket, up and down the cluster.

6 If shifts are slow when you shift from the smaller sprockets to the larger ones, tighten the cable tension. If they are slower in the other direction, slacken the cable tension.

brush. Once you have finished the cleaning stage, make sure you rinse it well so that no grit remains in any of the pivots. This component will then have to be set aside to dry. A quick way to remove water from the derailleur is to use electricians' switch-cleaner spray.

The rear derailleur is now ready to be reassembled. Take your new pulley wheels and spread grease over

both sides. Press a shim onto each side. Refit them, with the pulley cage half, to the main assembly and tighten the pulley bolts firmly.

Overhaul: Front derailleur
This device rarely requires anything more taxing than cleaning, which can be done without removing it from the frame. If you decide to remove the front derailleur, be sure to pos-

ition it correctly when you refit it to the frame. Only do this after the crankset has been fitted. Follow the method shown in the step-by-step photo sequence below.

Function check
It is important to give the gears a good function check by riding for a short distance, changing into each gear in turn as you travel along.

2 Slacken the clamp and move it up or down so that it clears the largest chainring by about ⅟₁₆in. on the sweep of its arc of travel.

3 Looking from above, rotate the derailleur so that the cage is parallel to the face of the outer chainring. Tighten the clamp lightly again.

4 Check these adjustments again before finally tightening the clamp firmly. The control cable can now be connected to the derailleur.

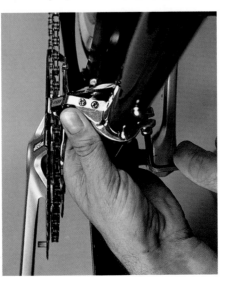

HUB GEARS

Function

Hub gears perform the same function as derailleur gears, but because they are fully enclosed within the rear hub, they do not suffer the effects of the elements. They do not provide as wide a range or choice of gears, but for many bicyclists they offer advantages over the more vulnerable derailleur systems. Hub gears are reliable, long-lasting and need little adjustment.

Check

While riding you will notice whether the gears are engaging properly or not, and clattering or grating noises coming from the hub indicate the latter. In many models, it is quite normal to hear a ticking sound when riding in some gears.

As with other hubs, the wheel bearings in a hub gear can come loose, and this should be checked as you would for a normal wheel.

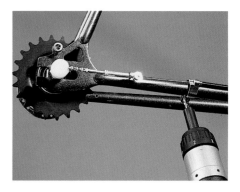

1 Check that the fulcrum clip is firmly anchored before you attempt to adjust the selector.

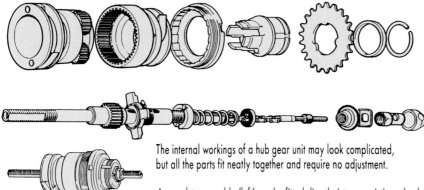

The internal workings of a hub gear unit may look complicated, but all the parts fit neatly together and require no adjustment.

A complete assembly (left) can be fitted directly into an existing wheel.

5 Tighten the adjuster until the shoulder on the selector is level with the end of the spindle.

▼ All hub gear systems (except the Sachs Orbit) use a wider chain than derailleur systems; these chains are joined with a spring link. This link is removed and replaced using a pair of pliers. Otherwise the chain is dealt with as with a derailleur chain. When the spring link is refitted, the rounded end should be pointing in the direction of the chain travel, or the spring link might come apart.

▼ Today, hub gears are sealed for lubrication. However, many models still in use will have a capped lubrication point in the hub shell. Place a few drops of SAE30 oil into this aperture every four to six weeks.

Service

Gear selector adjustments may have to be carried out several times after a new cable has been fitted. This is because the cable adjustment is critical to the proper functioning of the gears – and new cables tend to stretch. Eventually, the cable will be stretched to its limit, after which the gears will need no further adjustment until overhaul. Follow the method shown in the step-by-step photo sequence.

If there is a protective plastic end cap on the wheel nut, make sure that it is not fouling the selector chain. Simply turn the end cap slightly so that the chain has a clear run.

When adjusting the wheel bearings, it should be noted that the right-hand cone is pre-set at the factory; only the left-hand cone should

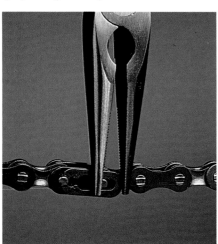

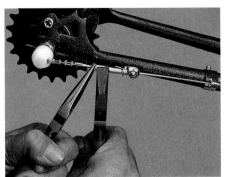

2 Set the gear lever to second gear if it is a three-speed gear, or to third if it is a five-speed.

3 Using two pairs of pliers, release the knurled lockring from the cable adjuster.

4 If one is fitted, make sure that the plastic end cap is not fouling the selector chain.

6 Check this adjustment by shining a light through the hole in the side of the wheel nut.

7 If it is not possible, the fulcrum clip must be moved forward or back along the chainstay.

8 When completed, tighten the locknut against the adjuster using two pairs of pliers.

be used to adjust the wheel bearings. You can undertake this job either with the wheel installed in the frame or, if you wish, with it removed. If the former is the case, first loosen the left-hand wheel nut, making sure that the right-hand wheel nut is tight. Take a pair of cone wrenches, and use one to slacken the locknut. Use the other to tighten the cone until it is hard against the ball bearings, then turn it back about one-eighth of a turn until a slight play is noticeable at the rim. Hold the cone in position with a cone wrench and tighten the locknut firmly up against it. Check the adjustment at the rim again and, if it is satisfactory, the wheel nut can be retightened.

If you choose to remove the wheel, the wheel spindle should be set into a vise with the hub's left-hand side uppermost. Be careful to avoid damaging the threads on the spindle. Now adjust it as per the instructions for making adjustments with the wheel installed.

Overhaul

You should only need to overhaul hub gears once every five years. Even then, a full overhaul should only be carried out if the routine maintenance fails to resolve any of the problems. Although it may be best to leave this task to your local bicycle store, it is, nevertheless, a most satisfying job to carry out, since each and every component part for a hub gear is available for renewal.

Sturmey Archer of America Inc., can supply a complete instruction guide for fully overhauling any of their products, which includes an exploded diagram showing the order codes for all the spare parts, and a comprehensive fault diagnosis chart.

Further information

Hub gears are available in a wide range of types. Three-, five- and seven-speed versions are available as simple hub gears, while other versions include a hub brake. Furthermore, geared hubs with integral coaster (or back-pedal) brakes are also manufactured. A derivative of the hub gear is the Orbit, from the manufacturer Sachs Huret, which combines a derailleur sprocket cluster with a two-speed hub gear.

If your bicycle features one of the combinations listed above, the maintenance and adjustment of the hub gears remains broadly the same as described here.

CONTROL LEVERS

Function

Control levers are usually fixed to the handlebar and allow you to operate gears or brakes comfortably and efficiently with your hands.

There are two basic types of brake lever: the hooded type designed especially for dropped handlebars, and the more common type designed for flat handlebars. These types are not interchangeable.

Gear shift controls come in three basic types. The most common has a revolving barrel which is turned by the shift lever. When the lever is operated with your finger, the cable wire is pulled around the barrel. This type includes the gear shift levers fitted to the end of dropped handlebars, and those found on the down tube of racing bicycles, as well as the most common position: on top of the handlebar, inboard of the handgrip. This type is occasionally found in the 'underbar' position, sometimes with a 'wishbone' lever.

Another popular type of gear control features two separate levers – one to shift down a gear, the other to shift up, with a marked click for each gear. This type is generally referred to as a 'rapid-fire' or 'push-push' shifter.

Lastly, and becoming increasingly popular, is the twistgrip type. As its name suggests, this mechanism is effectively a handlebar grip which is twisted to change from one gear to another, again with a distinct click for each gear shift.

Check: Brake controls

Brake levers should first be checked for comfort, especially on a new bicycle. On bicycles with flat handlebars, they should be positioned at a downwards angle that suits your riding position. On dropped handlebars, the levers should be positioned for comfort and to allow maximum movement of the operating lever.

Your brake levers must be secure on the handlebar. If the blade of the lever is bent or cracked, it must be replaced as soon as possible.

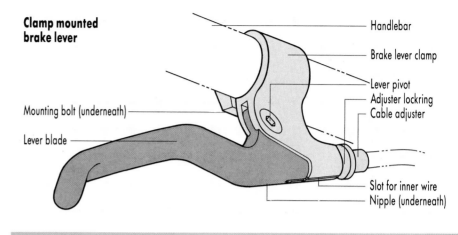

Clamp mounted brake lever

Handlebar

Brake lever clamp

Lever pivot

Adjuster lockring

Cable adjuster

Mounting bolt (underneath)

Lever blade

Slot for inner wire

Nipple (underneath)

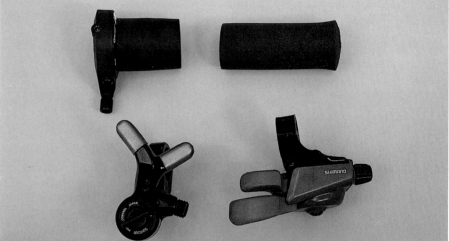

▲ Of the several types of twistgrip gear shifter (top), the 'Gripshift' is the most common. Barrel-type shifters come in a range of styles: for example, in an 'underbar' style (lower left). 'Push-push' shifters (lower right) are also popular.

▶ Brake levers with a clamp mounting are removed from the handlebar by loosening the mounting bolt, which is usually found on the underside.

Check: Gear controls

As with brake levers, gear shift controls should be positioned to provide maximum comfort and accessibility, and must also, of course, be secure on the handlebar.

The barrel type gear shift lever features a damper to counteract the effect of the relatively powerful return spring in the front or rear derailleur

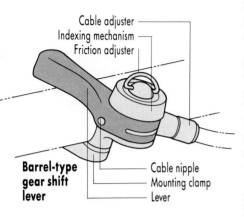

Cable adjuster
Indexing mechanism
Friction adjuster

Barrel-type gear shift lever

Cable nipple
Mounting clamp
Lever

Check to make sure that your levers are working freely but that the gears do not slip.

Service: Brake lever

The adjustments that need to be made to the brake levers are minimal. To set them in the best position and to secure them properly to the handlebars requires the same simple operation: a loosening of the clamp or band bolt as necessary.

With the majority of levers designed for flat handlebars, this bolt is located on the external part of the

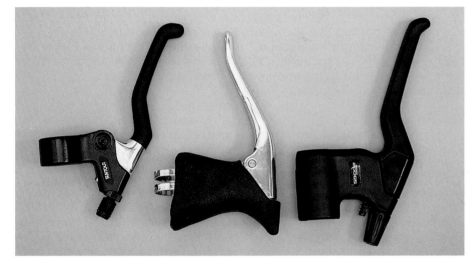

▲ Levers designed for flat bars (left) usually have a clamp fitting. Levers for dropped handlebars (center) have an inward-curving lever and a band-type fitting. Many bicycles today have a lever for flat bars with a band-type fitting (right).

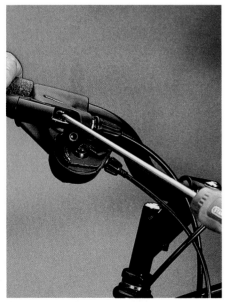

◀ Brake levers that feature a band-type fitting are removed by loosening the mounting-bolt, which is located inside the body of the lever.

clamp, usually on the underside of the main body. Hooded brake levers for dropped handlebars are secured to the handlebar by a band which is progressively tightened by the band bolt situated actually within the body of the lever. Access to this bolt is gained by operating the brake lever blade. The clamp bolt can then be seen beyond the cable wire.

Service: Gear shifter

All handlebar-mounted gear shift levers are secured by a clamp, and the bolt to adjust this will be found on the clamping part of the lever body.

Twistgrip-type gear shift controls vary from make to make and have few similarities. If your bicycle is fitted with these, you should seek specific instructions direct from the manufacturers themselves.

On the barrel type you should fine-tune the friction adjuster (either an integral finger-grip, or a fold-out D-shaped wire) until it is just right: too tight and gear shifts become stiff, too loose and the lever will not be able to hold the selected gear, because the spring in the derailleur will pull the cable back around the barrel.

Friction adjustment is not required with the push-push type of gear shift controls.

Overhaul

The simplicity of brake levers means that they generally give long-lasting, reliable service, requiring no more than a spot of lube on the pivot. In many designs, the brake lever blade is secured to the body with a nut and bolt, which can be removed for cleaning and regreasing. However, be careful to replace any shims and bushes that may be part of the assembly. When refitting the blade to the lever body, be sure to tighten it sufficiently to prevent it rattling – but leave it free enough to allow efficient control action.

While brake levers remain simple to maintain, gear shift controls have become more sophisticated, and many cannot be overhauled. This is particularly the case with the push-push type, where dismantling should not be attempted. Most other designs, however, can be partially dismantled for cleaning and lubricating purposes at least. On the whole, gear shifters function satisfactorily for a long time, but when they become unreliable through wear, they should be replaced as soon as possible.

CABLES

Function
The control cables on a bicycle allow the brakes and gears to be operated from the handlebar. These cables are comprised of an inner wire (which is stranded or braided), and an outer flexible casing, which is coiled and which covers the inner wire for some, or nearly all, of its length. In recent years, to meet the demands of indexed gear systems, a new type of outer casing, with a longitudinal structure (instead of a coiled one), has been developed.

A bicycle usually has four control cables. Two cables operate the brakes, and two the derailleurs. Brake cables are significantly thicker than derailleur cables because they have to cope with greater strains.

Check
The inner wire is quite flexible, but if it is forced to travel around too sharp a bend, or if it is allowed to rub, it will ultimately break. Pay close attention to any section of cable on either side of a guide-pulley. The pulleys are usually too small, and so force the wire to flex each time it is operated. Also pay attention to the point where the inner wire enters the outer casing, and to where the cable passes through a guide.

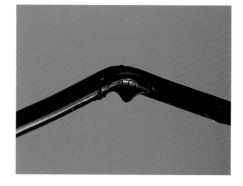

▲ If a control cable has been forced to take too tight a route, or if it is too short for the purpose, it will become kinked, and will split.

It is very important that the inner wire slides smoothly inside the outer casing. If it does not, it could indicate that there is no lubrication, or that the inner wire is kinked.

Service
There is little you can do to service a control cable. The usual, and safest, course of action is simply to renew it. In most cases, you will only need to renew the inner wire.

Overhaul
Even if your control cables appear to be functioning satisfactorily, it is wise to renew all inner wires as a matter

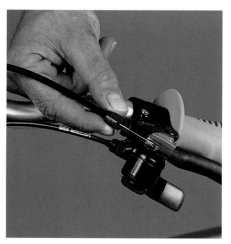

1 Slacken the lockring on the brake lever adjuster and screw the adjuster in as far as it will go. This provides slack in the cable. Note that the slots on the adjuster should be aligned.

of routine: simply remove the old wires and fit new ones. Follow the method shown in the photo sequences above (for brake cables) and below (for gear cables). To refit a cable, follow the procedures given below.

Brake cables
If you are renewing the inner wire only, then pull the old wire out of the casing, lubricate the new one with grease and slide it into the casing,

1 Close the gear lever against its stop, allowing the maximum amount of cable out of the lever.

Special tools:
Third-hand tool
Wire cutters

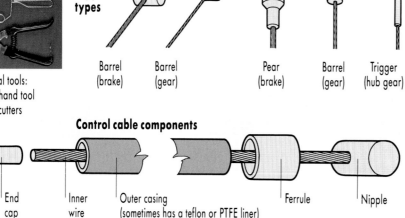

Nipple types

Barrel (brake) Barrel (gear) Pear (brake) Barrel (gear) Trigger (hub gear)

Control cable components

End cap | Inner wire | Outer casing (sometimes has a teflon or PTFE liner) | Ferrule | Nipple

2 Fit a third-hand tool over the brake blocks. This pushes them together to give further slack in the cable. Loosen the cable anchor bolt and withdraw the cable wire from the cable anchor.

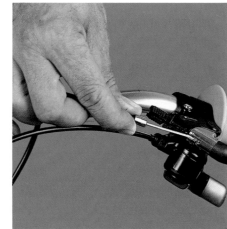

3 Slide the cable casing out of the lever adjuster, making sure the ferrules come out too. Move it sideways. The inner wire will pass through the slots when they are aligned.

4 Once the wire is at a right-angle to the lever, and aligned with the slot underneath the lever, the nipple can be pulled out of its housing in the lever, from below, to release the cable.

ensuring that all ferrules and lever covers are in place beforehand. Insert the nipple into the underside of the lever, and the wire into the slot in the adjuster. Settle the casing into the end of the adjuster. Feed the inner wire through the cable stop above the brake, and through the anchor bolt on the yoke, where it should be clamped fairly tightly, but not so tight that it crimps the wire. Remove the third-hand tool and adjust the cable

at the lever if necessary. Once you have fully adjusted the brakes, re-tighten the cable anchor bolt firmly, cut off any surplus wire and either fit a cap over the end, or apply a little Superglue to it. Both will prevent the end from splaying.

Derailleur cables
Fit a new cable by feeding the end through the aperture in the gear lever. Lubricate the wire with grease,

and feed it through the outer casing, and through the various guides, and then clamp it in the cable anchor with the anchor bolt. Adjust the derailleur according to the manufacturer's instructions, or follow the advice given previously. Finally, tighten the clamps and trim off the excess.

New cables nearly always stretch a little after being fitted. This is most noticeable with gear cables, because it affects the adjustment of the gears.

2 Loosen the cable anchor bolt on the derailleur and release the wire from the clamp.

3 Push the gear lever as far as it will go; this will begin to pull the wire out of the casing.

4 Close the lever again and the nipple will protrude. Draw it out of the casing through the lever body.

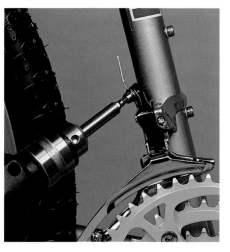

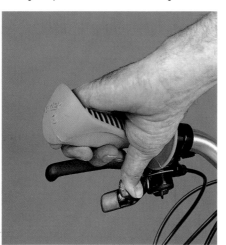

CANTILEVER BRAKES

Function

In basic terms, each brake block is attached to a pivoting assembly on either side of the wheel rim. When the brake lever is operated, the brake blocks close against the rim and thus slow the motion of the wheel.

Cantilever brakes are the type most frequently found on bicycles today. A few derivatives of the design gained some popularity for a few years, but these are no longer specified. The derivative designs utilized similar frame-mounted pivots. For our purposes, the principles for checking, servicing and overhauling these types are all broadly the same.

Check

First check that the cable tension provides the optimum braking effect. Test for this by pulling the brake lever against the handlebar. The lever should cease to move easily at about 1¼ in. or so from the handgrip. Now, pull hard: the lever should move another ⅝ in., or a little more. This additional movement represents the cable's 'take-up.' (Cable take-up is caused by: stretching of the inner wire, combined with a slight compression of the outer casing; flexing of the brake arms and brake bosses; and compression of the brake blocks.) With the lever in this position, you are able to apply maximum pressure to it with your fingers. If the brake lever cannot be pulled to within ⅝ in. of the handlebar, the cable tension should be slackened slightly. If you can pull the lever so that it touches

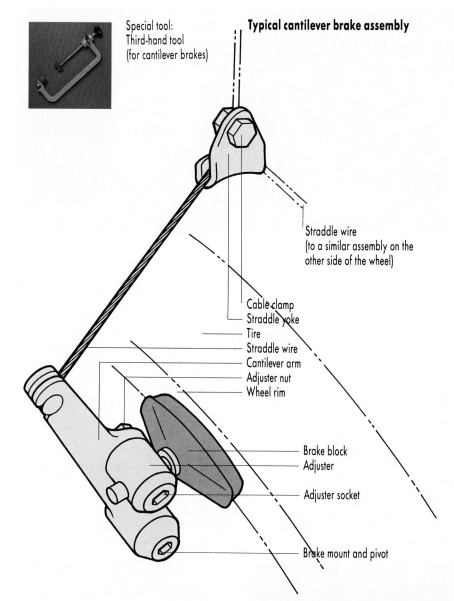

Special tool:
Third-hand tool
(for cantilever brakes)

Typical cantilever brake assembly

Straddle wire
(to a similar assembly on the other side of the wheel)

Cable clamp
Straddle yoke
Tire
Straddle wire
Cantilever arm
Adjuster nut
Wheel rim

Brake block
Adjuster

Adjuster socket

Brake mount and pivot

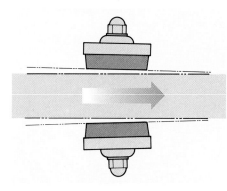

◀ To prevent the brake from squealing, each brake block should be positioned so that the trailing end closes onto the rim before the leading end by about ¹⁄₁₆ in. The trailing end of the brake is relative to rim travel, not bicycle travel.

▶ After disconnecting the cable, the brake cantilever assembly is removed from its boss by unscrewing and removing the pivot mounting bolt. The bolt can be screwed back into the boss to avoid loosing it. Don't forget to clean and regrease the pivot before refitting the brake assembly.

the handlebar, the cable tension should be tightened.

Now check that the brake blocks align with the rim. If the blocks close too high on the rim, they will rub the sidewalls of the tire, causing it to split. If they strike the rim too low, there is a risk that the brake blocks will slip past the rim. The latter will lead either to total brake failure, or to the brake blocks' being caught in the spokes – with dramatic consequences for the rider.

Check also that the brake blocks do not rub on the rim when the brake is not in operation – this is called 'binding'. If the brake squeals when applied, the brake blocks need to be toed-out.

Also check that the braking sur-faces are clean and free of all con-taminants, especially if you ride mainly on city streets.

If, when you check your brake blocks, you find that they are worn down, they must be replaced. Some brake blocks feature a wear line, which indicates when they should be replaced. It is most important to take note of this because the brake block is molded around a metal shoe. If this shoe is allowed to wear to the surface of the block, it will slice into your rims and wreck them in no time at all.

Service
The brake blocks are mounted so that they can be adjusted in all planes, and are secured in position with the adjusting nut. On the front of the brake assembly is an Allen socket into which you can insert an Allen wrench to help you align the brake block. This socket has no tightening or loos-ening function.

To adjust your brake blocks, fol-low the method shown in the step-by-step photo sequence. This is not as easy as it looks, because the block has a tendency to move slightly as you finally tighten the adjusting nut. With experience, you will learn to anticipate this. Nevertheless, you may need to make a couple of attempts to get the position just right.

At the same time, to prevent the brake from squealing when applied, each brake block should be posi-tioned so that the trailing end closes onto the rim before the leading end by roughly $\frac{1}{16}$ in. Identify the trailing and leading ends from the diagram (left, on page 60). The trailing end is usually toward the front, except when the brake is mounted on the chainstays, in which case it is toward the ground.

Removal
After disconnecting the cable, remove the brake cantilever assembly from its boss by unscrewing the securing bolt. The bolt should be wired to the cantilever assembly so that it is not lost. Alternatively, you can simply screw the bolt back into the boss.

Overhaul
Overhauling cantilever brakes involves dismantling the assembly so that the brake blocks can be renewed, or cleaned with emery cloth. Prior to refitting, the pivot on the mounting bolt should be regreased. Once refit-ted, the brake blocks should be adjusted for alignment as above.

Brake blocks
There are several brands of brake block which are formulated for enhanced braking effect. You may choose to fit a set of these in place of the blocks supplied with your bicycle.

1 Using finger pressure, push the brake block up against the rim. Assess which way it must be adjusted to align with the rim.

2 Insert an Allen wrench into the socket on the front and, with a ring wrench, loosen the adjusting nut on the back approximately one full turn.

3 Maneuver the brake block with the Allen wrench until it is in the correct position, then tighten the adjusting nut sufficiently to hold it.

4 Push the brake block back up against the rim to check the results of your adjustment. If satisfactory, tighten the adjusting nut firmly.

HUB BRAKES

Function

Hub brakes are operated in the same way as other brakes – by pulling the brake levers on the handlebar. With hub brakes, however, a pair of curved shoes are expanded onto the inside of the hub shell. Like hub gears, they benefit from being enclosed within the hub and thus do not suffer the effects of the elements.

A popular alternative hub brake, for the rear wheel only, is a coaster (or back-pedal) brake. It operates when the pedals are turned backward, which activates a brake mechanism inside the hub.

Check: Hub brakes

Few problems will be encountered with hub brakes. The checks you make relate to cable adjustment. To make sure that the brake is being fully operated, pull the brake lever in toward the handlebar. You should easily be able to pull it to about 1¼ in. or so from the handgrip. If you then pull it hard, the lever should move a further ⅝ in. or so. This extra movement shows the amount of cable 'take-up'. With the lever at this distance from the handgrip, your hand is able to exert maximum power for effective braking. If this lever position cannot be achieved, the cable should be adjusted accordingly.

Also carry out a check to make sure that the brake is not binding, by lifting the wheel off the ground and spinning it. Listen carefully for a rubbing sound from the hub, and see if the wheel comes to rest gradually, after a number of oscillations, with the valve near the bottom. A rubbing sound, or the wheel suddenly grinding to a stop, are indications that the brake is binding.

As with other hubs, the bearing cone adjustment should be checked

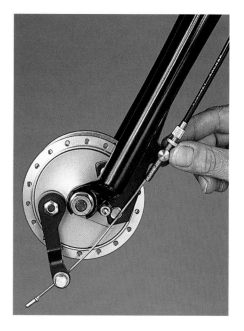

1 Unscrew the lockring a small amount and screw the adjuster down by a number of turns.

The workings of a hub brake

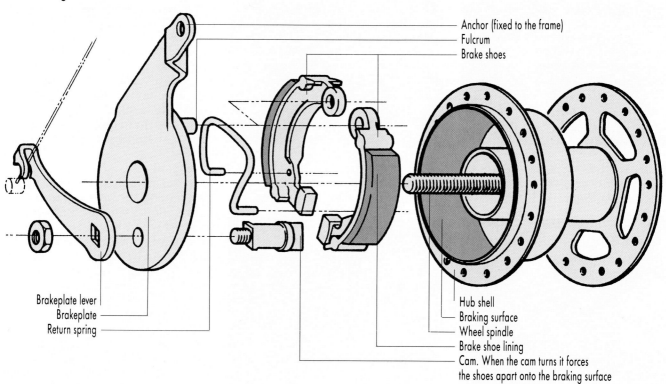

Anchor (fixed to the frame)
Fulcrum
Brake shoes

Brakeplate lever
Brakeplate
Return spring

Hub shell
Braking surface
Wheel spindle
Brake shoe lining
Cam. When the cam turns it forces the shoes apart onto the braking surface

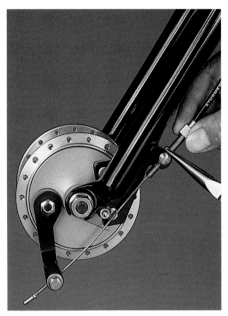

2 Spin the wheel and slowly unscrew the adjuster until you hear the brake shoes binding.

3 Screw the adjuster down again until the wheel turns freely and you no longer hear it binding.

4 Making sure that the adjuster stays in position, tighten the lockring against the adjuster.

regularly in the usual way, by looking for lateral movement at the rim.

The shoes of a hub brake can become contaminated because of careless lubrication, or if one of the internal oil seals begins to leak. When this occurs, the brake will cease to function effectively. This will usually be accompanied by loud, vibrating squeals when you apply the brakes. Contaminated shoes must be replaced with new ones.

Check: Coaster brakes
Back-pedal brakes are popular because they are very efficient and need virtually no maintenance. However, older models can become dry internally, and this is identified by a harsh or noisy braking action. If this is the case, the hub will need to be dismantled and repacked with grease. If you feel confident enough, this job can be attempted in your workshop at home – but, unless you have the full technical details of your particular model, it is perhaps best to ask the professional at your local bicycle store to do it.

Service: Hub and coaster brakes
Coaster brakes require no servicing, and hub brakes simply require occasional control cable adjustment with the wheel installed, but raised off the ground. Follow the method shown in the step-by-step photo sequence.

The cones on a hub brake should be adjusted as you would an ordinary hub. See pages 68 and 69 for further information on this.

Overhaul: Hub brakes
The hub brake bearings should be overhauled every six months, or at least every year, depending on the amount you use your bicycle. Refer to pages 68 and 69 for further advice on this topic.

However, the hub brakes themselves should only need attention every three to five years, again depending on how heavily they are used. The overhaul involves replacing the brake shoe assembly, which is a simple operation easily carried out by your bicycle store, if you choose not to do it yourself. It is wise to refer to the manufacturer's

technical information before embarking on the task yourself. Here is a brief description of what is involved.

Disconnect the cable from the brakeplate lever and, on the rear brake, remove the brake anchor arm bolt. Remove the wheel from the bicycle and mount it in a vise with the brakeplate uppermost. Remove the brakeplate retaining nut and the cone adjusting washer to release the brakeplate. Mount the brakeplate assembly firmly in the vise. Undo the brakeplate lever nut and remove the brakeplate lever. Remove the brake shoes from the fulcrum pin. In some designs this is facilitated by removing a circlip; in others, by undoing a bolt on the outside of the brake plate assembly. The brake shoe assembly can now be removed and a new one duly installed.

Refit the fulcrum circlip or bolt and reassemble the hub brake in reverse order to that described above. Remember that new hub-brake shoes usually take a while to 'bed in', during which time they will not be working at maximum efficiency.

SIDEPULL BRAKES

Function
Sidepull brakes act on the rim with brake blocks in a similar way to cantilever brakes, except that they have a single central pivot. The name derives from the arms of the brake calipers, which extend to the same side of the bicycle. When the brake lever is operated, the calipers are pulled together, and the brake blocks are squeezed against the rims.

Check
First check that the cable adjustment is correct. Grip the handlebar and gently pull the brake lever, as if you were operating the brake. You should be able to pull the lever to about 1¼ in. from the handgrip with ease.

Then a stronger pull on the lever should bring it to within about ⅝ in. of the handgrip. The difference between the two movements represents 'take-up', caused partly by cable stretch. With the brake lever about ⅝ in. or so from the handlebar, you are able to apply the maximum pressure to the brake.

Check the alignment of the brake blocks with the rim. They should not strike it too low, which will reduce braking effectiveness, and cause the blocks to wear unevenly and rapidly. Nor should they strike it too high, or they will rub the sidewall of the tire and cause a split.

Check that the brake blocks clear the rim and do not bind, and that the

1 Push the brake block against the rim with your fingers. Decide if it needs to be moved up or down.

calipers are centered over the wheel.

Check that the brake assembly is firm in its mounting, and that the brake calipers pivot freely. Neither should they be sloppy.

Further reductions in braking efficiency can be the result of the braking surfaces of the brake blocks becoming contaminated with road grime. A greasy cocktail is picked up off the road by your wheels and sprayed over the brakes. Regular and frequent cleaning of the blocks is important to maintain efficiency.

Regularly check your brake blocks

▼ The sidepull brake assembly is removed by removing the mounting nut and withdrawing the pivot bolt. The mounting bolt should be tightly secured, but if there is still some play in the calipers, check the pivot nut and locknut on the front.

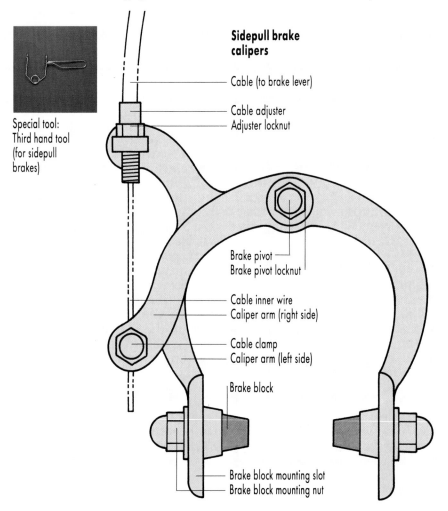

Special tool: Third hand tool (for sidepull brakes)

Sidepull brake calipers

- Cable (to brake lever)
- Cable adjuster
- Adjuster locknut
- Brake pivot
- Brake pivot locknut
- Cable inner wire
- Caliper arm (right side)
- Cable clamp
- Caliper arm (left side)
- Brake block
- Brake block mounting slot
- Brake block mounting nut

2 Loosen the retaining nut and move the brake block until it is aligned.

3 Steady the brake block with an adjustable wrench and tighten the retaining nut.

4 Check the toe-out and use an adjustable wrench gently to twist the mounting slot.

for wear; some blocks are marked with a wear line, and it is very important to keep an eye on this. Modern brake blocks are molded around a metal shoe and when the block exceeds its wear life, this shoe will break through the surface of the block. As most rims today are made of alloy, the shoe, which is made from steel, will cut into your rims very quickly. You will then have to replace the rims as well.

Service
If the lever cannot be brought close enough to the handgrip, the cable tension should be slackened slightly. However, if the lever touches the handlebar when pulled, the cable needs to be tightened.

The brake blocks are mounted in

a slot so that they can be adjusted up or down in relation to the rim. Follow the method shown in the photo sequence.

To prevent the brake from squealing when applied, the brake block mounting must be physically twisted using an adjustable wrench, so that the trailing end closes onto the rim before the leading end. This must be done with some care to avoid damaging the brake caliper.

If the brake blocks are binding, first center the assembly over the wheel, using a hammer and drift. If they are still binding once you have centered the calipers, the cable tension should be slackened.

If there is any play in the assembly, tighten the pivot on its mounting by turning the brake mounting nut. If

this is tightly secured already, then the brake caliper retaining nut should be tightened down and the locknut secured against it.

Removal
Remove sidepull brakes from their mountings by unscrewing the brake mounting nut and sliding out the pivot bolt, complete with the whole brake assembly.

Overhaul
Mount the pivot bolt in the vise. Remove the brake arm retaining nut along with the locknut. Prepare to remove the bush washers, calipers and return spring from the pivot bolt. Take each item off the pivot bolt, noting the exact order in which each item comes off. Lay these items out in the correct order. Clean each part and spread grease over the pivot bolt. Refit each part onto the pivot bolt in the correct order, refit the return spring, the calipers and the bushing washers. Tighten the brake retaining nut so there is little play in the arms. Tighten the locknut against the retaining nut, testing the brake arms to see that they pivot freely without any play at all. The overhauled brake assembly is now ready to be reinstalled on the bicycle.

Sometimes, when the brake mounting nut is tightened, the whole brake assembly tends to turn with the nut, causing one brake block to rub on the rim all the time. This is best, and quickly, solved by giving the return spring a sharp blow at a point very near to the pivot on the side that is not rubbing. Use a metal hammer and drift, and check after each blow to see if the brake is centered: start with a gentle tap and increase the impact as necessary.

FREEWHEEL

Function

The rear hub is equipped with a set of drive sprockets, mounted on a freewheel, which carry the chain and turn the rear wheel.

The freewheel allows you to stop pedaling from time to time (hence the term 'freewheeling'). There are two types of freewheel body: a screw-on freewheel, as the name implies, is screwed onto the hub, while a cassette freewheel, again as the name implies, is integral with the hub.

Check

To check the freewheel, slowly turn the sprockets counterclockwise. You should hear a regular clicking, but listen for grating sounds or irregularity in the clicking. Check to see that they rotate freely without any play.

Service

Neither the screw-on nor the cassette types of freewheel are serviceable. If there is a problem, they have to be overhauled, or renewed.

Overhaul

A freewheel overhaul requires special tools and skills, so you may prefer to leave this job to a bicycle store. However, you may occasionally want to

▼ Some Shimano and Campagnolo cassette freewheels have a small retaining lockring which holds the sprockets onto the splines. A special tool is required to remove it.

remove the sprockets from the freewheel body, or the screw-on freewheel body from the hub.

Removing sprockets

It is best to remove the sprockets while the freewheel is fixed to the wheel. Place the wheel on the floor, leaning against a wall, and follow the method shown in the step-by-step photo sequence.

In most cases, the second-smallest sprocket will unscrew along with the smallest, and the remaining sprockets will then slide off. In other cases, the third or fourth sprocket will also have to be unscrewed.

Removing a screw-on freewheel

It is essential to use the correct

Special Tools:
Freewheel remover
Cassette ring remover
Chain whips

1 Looking at the freewheel, wrap the loose section of chain on one chainwhip around the third sprocket in a counterclockwise direction and engage the fixed section of chain.

Freewheel bodies

The two types are shown with the sprockets removed

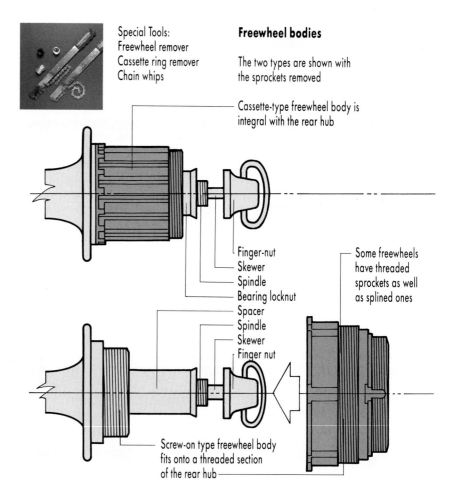

Cassette-type freewheel body is integral with the rear hub

Finger-nut
Skewer
Spindle
Bearing locknut
Spacer
Spindle
Skewer
Finger nut

Some freewheels have threaded sprockets as well as splined ones

Screw-on type freewheel body fits onto a threaded section of the rear hub

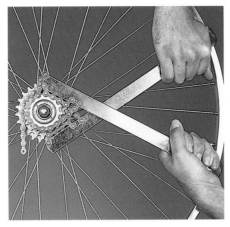

2 Take the other chainwhip and wrap it around the smallest sprocket in the opposite direction. The handles of the chainwhips should cross over each other when you do this.

3 Hold the wheel between your legs and, using both hands, squeeze the handles together until the smallest sprocket begins to unscrew. Be careful not to pinch your fingers.

4 Unwrap the chainwhips and unscrew the smallest sprocket by hand. Once removed, the remaining sprockets should slide off. Be sure to note the order in which the spacers come off.

removing tool. This will be specific, not only to the make of freewheel, but sometimes to the type as well. Ask your local bicycle store.

Once you have removed your wheel from the bicycle, unscrew the wheel nut from the freewheel side and slip the freewheel removing tool over the spindle, and replace the

▼ Use the bench vise to remove a freewheel – it gives you better purchase and is safer.

wheel nut, tightening it by hand only. Alternatively, if your bicycle has quick-release spindles (see pages 68 and 69), unscrew the nut and draw the skewer out of the spindle. Slip the freewheel removing tool over the spindle and replace the quick-release skewer. Lightly tighten the nut, and put the quick-release lever into the closed position, making sure it is not too tight.

Unscrew the freewheel in a coun-

terclockwise direction. Mount the wheel in the vise, ensuring that the vise jaws close firmly on the flats of the freewheel-removing-tool. Grasp the wheel at the rim and turn it to unscrew the freewheel.

As soon as you feel the freewheel begin to give, stop unscrewing, undo the wheel nut slightly, then start unscrewing again. Repeat this process until the freewheel can be unscrewed by hand.

HUBS

Function

The hubs are located at the center of the wheels, and they house the bearings for the wheel. The standard hub, which is secured to the frame drop-outs with wheel nuts, is being gradually superseded on new models by the quick-release hub.

With quick-release hubs you do not need a wrench to remove the wheel. They have a hollow spindle, through which a skewer runs. At one end of the skewer there is an adjusting finger-nut; at the other there is a lever-operated cam. When the quick-release lever is put into the closed position, the cam turns within its housing and pushes the housing up against the drop-out. This in turn pulls the adjusting finger-nut at the other end up against the other drop-out.

To release the wheel from the frame, the quick-release lever is moved into the open position (the brake cable may have to be released as well). For safety reasons, many new bicycles are fitted with drop-outs that have a lip on the lower edge. The lip prevents the wheel from coming out of the frame if the quick-release is accidentally opened. Indeed, the wheel may not come out even if the quick-release lever is deliberately opened. When this is the case, the wheel has to be released by gripping the adjusting finger-nut, setting the lever into the open position and, using the lever as a handle, unwinding the quick-release housing until the wheel can come away from the frame.

Check

To see whether the bearings are too tight, mount the bicycle in the work-stand, turn the wheel very slowly and then let it go. When checking the rear

1 Before adjusting the quick-release, make sure that the wheel easily fits into the frame by releasing the brake cable.

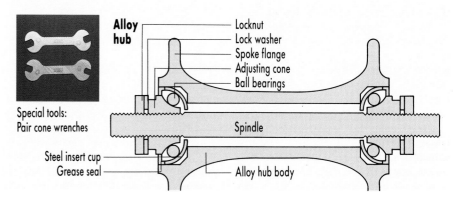

Special tools:
Pair cone wrenches

Alloy hub

Locknut
Lock washer
Spoke flange
Adjusting cone
Ball bearings
Spindle
Steel insert cup
Grease seal
Alloy hub body

1 Mount the spindle in the vise. Use vise clamps to avoid damaging the thread. Unscrew the upper locknut and cone. Pick out the ball bearings using tweezers, and put them into a container.

2 Hold the upper end of the spindle and lift the wheel out of the vise by the spindle. Lower the hub over the top of the container and let go of the spindle. Clean all the parts.

3 When all the parts are clean and dry, mount the spindle in the vise and smear grease into both bearing cups. Use tweezers to put ball bearings around the inside of each cup.

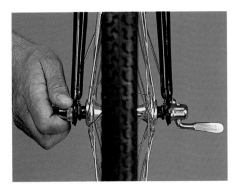

2 With the quick-release lever in the open position, do up the adjusting nut until it is tight, then undo it by half a turn.

3 To make sure that it is fully clamped when the lever is in the closed position, the lever should require a distinct force to close it.

4 You should not now need to alter the adjustment if you simply open the lever to remove the wheel. Position it so it cannot accidentally come open.

wheel, the chain must be disengaged. Note how the wheel rotates first in one direction, then in another, finally coming to rest with the valve near the bottom. If it stops suddenly, or you can hear a grating sound coming from the hub, the bearing is too tight.

To see whether the bearing is too loose, hold the rim near the chain-stay and, using the chainstay as a fixed point, try to move the rim from side to side. If any movement can be felt,

4 Lower the hub over the spindle with extreme care. Screw the cone onto the spindle and hand-tighten, then fit the lock washer and locknut. Adjust as you would for a service.

the bearing is loose. A sideways movement can also be a symptom of a loosely adjusted quick-release mechanism, so follow the step-by-step photo sequence above to check that this is not the cause before assuming that the bearings are loose.

Service: Standard hub
The bearing can be adjusted with the wheel in place. Unscrew one wheel nut a few turns (the nut on either side of the front wheel, that on the left side of the rear wheel). Slot one cone wrench onto the locknut and another onto the cone flats. Loosen the locknut and adjust the cone until the wheel has a very slight play at the rim. Be careful not to confuse the movement you will feel because the wheel is clamped on one side only, with looseness in the bearing. When you are satisfied with the adjustment, tighten the locknut up against the cone, tighten the wheel nut and check to see whether the adjustment is now satisfactory.

Service: Quick-release hub
Again, the bearing can be adjusted with the wheel installed. Open the quick-release lever and grasp the finger-nut at the other end of the spindle. Using the quick-release lever, tighten the quick-release mechanism into the finger-nut as tightly as it will go. But leave the quick-release lever

in the open position. The wheel is now clamped to the drop-out on one side only. Working on the same side as the quick-release lever, adjust the hub bearing as described above. When you are satisfied with the adjustment, loosen the finger nut and follow the photo sequence above until the quick-release mechanism functions properly.

Overhaul
Following the photo sequence (below left), mount the wheel horizontally in the bench vise, making sure that the vise jaws close onto the flats of the locknut if yours is a quick-release hub. Be very careful to avoid damaging the thread.

Note that the bearing cups are fitted inside the hub body. These should be cleaned in place. Once all the parts of the hub have been dismantled, check them for wear, especially the cones and cups. Once cleaned, the races where the ball bearings run should be bright and smooth. If they are dull and pitted, they need to be renewed. Check the old ball bearings against the new ones to make sure you have the right size.

When refitting a wheel with a standard hub, you simply need to make sure that the wheel nuts are tight. If yours has a quick-release hub, follow the method shown in the step-by-step photo sequence above.

SPOKES & RIMS

Function
Along with the hub, the spokes and rim make up the wheel assembly. Although wheel-building is a skilled craft, the amateur bicyclist can quite easily maintain wheels in a safe condition. This involves tightening loose spokes, relieving any slight wobbles and replacing broken spokes. It is advisable, however, to take your wheels to your local bicycle store occasionally so they can 'true' them.

Check
Spokes can be checked for even tension while the wheel is still mounted in the bicycle. Grasp a pair of spokes on each side of the wheel, using the index finger and thumb of each hand. Squeeze the spokes together, feeling for any marked differences in tension. Begin this process at the valve and carefully work your way right around the wheel until you get back to the valve again.

Closely inspect the rim for dents and distortion caused by any impacts – especially after a crash. After that, spin the whole wheel around to check for any wobbles. Although not

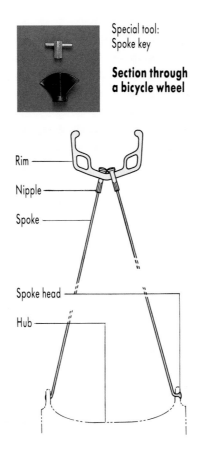

Special tool:
Spoke key

Section through a bicycle wheel

Rim

Nipple

Spoke

Spoke head

Hub

1 The wheel should be mounted in the bicycle. Rotate it slowly. Hold a stick of chalk steady against the fork or seatstay, and gradually bring it closer to the rim as the wheel spins.

dangerous in themselves, wobbles will interfere with rim brake operation.

When removing the tire and tube, the spoke ends should be checked to see that they don't protrude through the rim so far that they could puncture the tube. If your rim is made of steel, check inside for rust. This should be cleaned with a wire brush and treated with a rust inhibitor that will not attack rubber.

1 Feed the new spoke through the spoke hole in the hub, making sure that the spoke head is the right way round, following the pattern.

2 Weave it in and out of the existing spokes, working gradually toward the new spoke's hole in the rim. Don't worry about bending it.

3 When deciding whether to weave inside or outside, follow the same pattern as the other spokes, over and under.

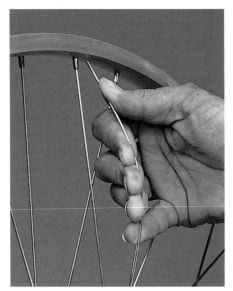

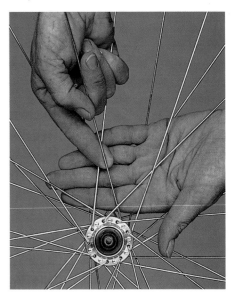

2 If there are any sideways deflections from true, the chalk will mark them. It is at these points that you should tighten or loosen spokes to bring the wheel back into trueness.

3 Identify the spoke nearest to the point of maximum deflection. If it goes to the same side as the chalk mark, it should be loosened, and if to the opposite, it should be tightened.

4 If the deflection covers a number of spokes, the same principle of tightening and loosening applies – same-side spokes should be loosened, opposite-side spokes should be tightened.

Service

If you find any loose spokes, simply tighten them until they are at more or less the same tension as all the other spokes. Once you have taken up any slack in the loose spokes, the wheel is ready to be checked for trueness. Follow the method shown in the step-by-step photo sequence above. Each adjustment should be slight – just a half-turn at a time.

Overhaul

Remove the wheel from the bicycle, and the tire and tube from the wheel. If you find a broken spoke, you will need to measure the spoke length of your wheel as accurately as possible. Take the measurement from the center of the spoke head at one end to the nipple at the other, then add on 7/16 in. for the nipple. Take the remains of the old spoke to your local

bicycle store to ensure you get a new spoke of the correct gauge. Even if they don't have one of the right length in stock, they will be able to cut and re-thread one for you.

To fit a new spoke, follow the method shown in the step-by-step photo sequence below. Having replaced any broken spokes and taken up the slack, the wheel is ready to be checked for trueness at the bicycle store.

4 Once you have woven it correctly, you will be able to feed it through the spoke hole in the rim and put a nipple through the rim onto the end.

5 You can take up the slack quickly by using a screwdriver in the slot in the nipple. Be careful to avoid over-tightening at this stage.

6 Now you can tension the spoke using a spoke wrench. Once it is at about the right tension, you can check the wheel for wobbles.

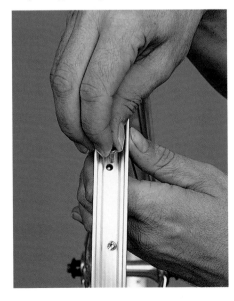

TIRES & TUBES

Function

Tires provide both a degree of suspension for your bicycle and grip for your wheels. The inner tube holds the air inside the tire.

Check

Close inspection of the tire will reveal the state of the tread, which should be in good condition to provide grip. Also look out for (and remove) any stones or fragments of glass embedded in the tread. If the tire is old, but has not been used much, it may have become perished. Check this by deflating the tire and pinching the carcass. If the surface of the rubber is crazed with ozone cracks, the tire is finished and should be replaced as soon as possible.

Check the sidewalls for splits or fraying of the carcass. Spin the wheel to see if the tire wobbles on the rim. If it does so, the tire is not seated properly. Check that the seating line is parallel to the rim all the way around. Make sure that the valve is seated properly by checking that it is perpendicular to the rim, and that the bead is seated correctly.

1 Deflate the tire and pinch it all the way around so the bead is in the trough of the rim. Hook a tire lever under the bead, in line with the first spoke from the valve.

Service

If the tire tread is worn, you should make a note to renew it at the next overhaul. If there is a split in the sidewall, the tire must be replaced with a new one immediately.

If you find that your tire is not seated properly, simply deflate the tire. Pinch it all around, pulling the sidewall away from the rim. At the same time you can align the valve so that it is perpendicular by moving the

26 x 1.15 26 x 1.25 26 x 1.4 26 x 1.5 26 x 1.75 26 x 1.8 26 x 1.95 26 x 2.0 26 x 2.125 26 x 2.2 26 x 2.25 26 x 2.5	These tire sizes denote common mountain or cross-bike tires, which use a 559mm (22in.) bead-seat diameter.
26 x 1⅜ 26 x 1⅜ x 1¼ 650A 26 x 1½	These sizes denote old 'roadster' tires, which use a 590mm (24 in.) bead-seat diameter.
700 x 18C 700 x 20C 700 x 23C 700 x 25C 28C x 28C 700 x 32C 700 x 35C 700 x 37C	These sizes denote 'French Standard' road or cross-bike tires, which use a 622mm (24½ in.) bead-seat diameter.
27 x ⅞ 27 x 1 27 x 1⅛ 27 x 1¼ 27 x 1⅜ 27 x 1½	These sizes denote 'English Standard' road bike tires, which use a 630mm (24¾ in.) bead-seat diameter.

When selecting new tires, look for the bead-seat diameter marking: 559, 590, 622, 630.

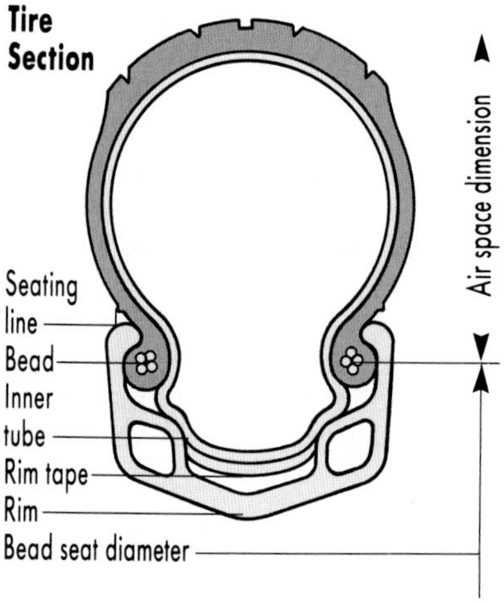

Tire Section

Seating line
Bead
Inner tube
Rim tape
Rim
Bead seat diameter

Air space dimension

1 Roll one bead of the tire over the rim all around. Remove the collar on the valve stem, and, pulling back the tire, push it through the rim. Pump a small amount of air into the tube.

2 Stuff the tube into the tire, making sure there are no twists or kinks in the tube. Starting opposite the valve, begin rolling the bead over the rim using your thumbs, working both ways.

2 Hook two more levers under the bead in line with the next but one spoke, on either side of the first lever. Pull each lever down, one by one, and hook it around the spoke.

3 As you pull the last lever down, the middle lever will fall out as the bead pops over the rim. Slide one of the remaining levers all the way around to release the bead.

4 Remove the collar on the valve stem and push the valve through the rim. Withdraw the tube. The other bead can now be removed from the rim with your fingers.

tire one way or the other around the rim of the wheel.

To make quite sure that the tire will seat properly, you can paint soapy water all around where the tire and rim meet. Pump up the tire until it is soft and push the valve into the valve hole so that the base of the valve is pushed past the bead of the tire. Now, take the weight off the wheel and inflate the tire until it is hard, checking that the seat line is parallel

to the rim while you do so. If the tire will not seat properly after this, you will have to remove it and carefully check the bead all around, to see if it has a kink. Straighten it as you would any piece of bent wire.

If you have had to remove any glass fragments from the tread, place a drop of Superglue in the resulting split(s). This will extend your tire's life, but be sure to check it carefully each week anyway.

Overhaul
Remove the tire and tube by following the method shown in the step-by-step photo sequence above.

Over a period of time, a certain amount of dust and water will creep inside the tire. To counter the effects of this, clean both the inside and outside of the tire with warm soapy water, looking for any stones and glass fragments that have worked right into the carcass and which may be protruding right inside the tire. Clean the tube as well. Wipe both and hang them up to dry. When they are thoroughly dry, lightly dust both the inner tube and the inside of the tire with talcum powder.

To extend the life of your tires, change them from wheel to wheel from time to time. That is, fit the front tire to the back wheel, and vice versa. This will equalize the wear between the two, because the rear tire tends to wear faster than the front one. This way you won't be left with one tire that is completely worn, and another that remains in quite good condition.

Refitting a tire requires more skill than removing one. Follow the method shown in the step-by-step photo sequence (left).

3 Work toward the valve, ensuring that where the bead is over the rim, it is well-seated into the trough of the rim. As you approach the valve, proceed in shorter stages.

4 As you reach the valve, the bead will become quite tight, but will finally plop over the rim. Push the valve in so that the valve seat is pushed past the beads. Inflate the tire.

PUNCTURES

Punctures need not be the problem many people imagine them to be. Before mending a puncture, you will have to remove the tire as shown on pages 72-73.

It is sometimes possible to find the approximate location of the puncture by pumping up the tire and listening carefully for the hiss of escaping air. Then you simply have to remove that part of the tire and extract the section of inner tube that is punctured. This technique is most useful for repairing punctures which occur when you are on the road, when you do not have access to your workshop tools and facilities.

You must follow the procedure shown in the step-by-step photo sequence very closely; there are no shortcuts. Once you have used this method a few times, it should take no more than a few minutes to repair a puncture effectively.

If you have difficulty finding the puncture, run the inflated inner tube through a bowl of water, section by section. However small the puncture, its location will be clearly indicated by a stream of bubbles.

1 To find a puncture hole, first pump some air into the inner tube and run it past your ear, section by section. Listen very carefully for the hiss of escaping air, and feel for a cooling air-flow against the sensitive skin on your cheek.

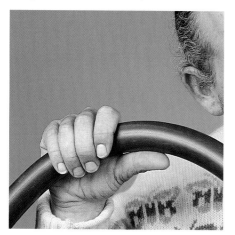

2 As you detect the location, put out your tongue and use it to pinpoint the puncture: you will feel the air on your tongue as it escapes. With the tip of your tongue, put a spot of saliva on the exact spot, and bubbles will show it up.

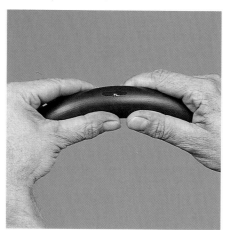

3 Use a piece of sandpaper, or emery cloth to clean as well as roughen the surface all around the puncture. Rub over an area larger than the size of the patch. Once finished, the rubber should look dull. Blow away any dust.

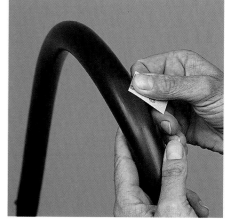

4 Keep some air in the inner tube and smear a very thin amount of rubber cement over the area. The escaping air will now show the puncture as a small white dot. Wait for a minute or two for the cement to become dry.

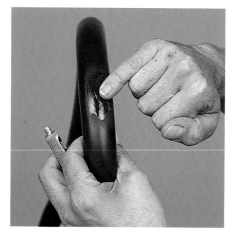

5 Remove the foil backing on the patch and stick it on the tube, right over the hole. Press it down firmly while releasing any remaining air in the tube. Peel away the protective cellophane, working from the center outward.

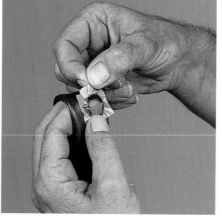

6 Pump some air into the tube and listen very carefully for escaping air, to make sure the repair is good. The whole area should now be dusted with talcum powder to prevent the tube from sticking to the inside of the tire.

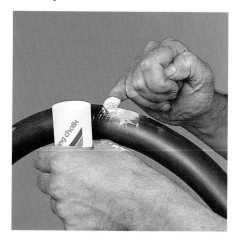

FENDERS

Function
If you use your bicycle regularly, the need for fenders is obvious. Not only do they protect the rider from tire spray; they also protect the bicycle from harmful, corrosive road spray. Fenders are not usually fitted to new bicycles today – and when they are, they may be rather short. They can be rendered more effective by fitting a mudflap.

Check
It is very important that all the fender stays are securely tightened. If a fender stay comes loose and entangles with the derailleur, it can cause much irreparable damage. A loose stay entangling the front wheel could cause you personal injury. The first indication of looseness is rattling, and this will be heard while you are riding along.

Also check that stays are not rubbing on the tire, because this will cause wear, or worse. Lift the wheel off the ground and spin it, listening carefully for any rubbing noise. As the wheel slows down, you will be able to locate exactly where the problem lies.

Service
In most cases the remedy for rattles is simply to tighten a nut or bolt. Sometimes it may also be necessary to wedge the joint, and a well-placed matchstick will usually do the trick. Also examine the mounting bracket on the rear brake bridge. The bracket is generally crimped with pliers around the sides of the fender, and may need recrimping, or replacing altogether.

If the fender is rubbing, it may be possible to bend and manipulate the stay so that it clears the tire. This will only solve the problem temporarily, however, and a better remedy is to undo the clamp nut and move the fender bracket up or down the fender stay. It is very often necessary to adjust the corresponding stay on the other side as well.

Fender mountings

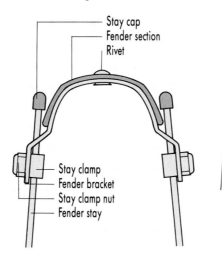

- Stay cap
- Fender section
- Rivet
- Stay clamp
- Fender bracket
- Stay clamp nut
- Fender stay

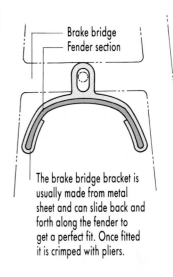

- Brake bridge
- Fender section

The brake bridge bracket is usually made from metal sheet and can slide back and forth along the fender to get a perfect fit. Once fitted it is crimped with pliers.

Removal
If all the stays are adjusted properly, it is best to remove the fenders (once the wheels have been removed from the bicycle) by undoing the mounting bolts in the mounting eyes on the frame and forks, and leaving the stay clamp bolts alone. Once these fixings are free, you can then undo the remaining mounting points. These will be found on the fork crown for the front wheel, and on the brake bridge and chainstay bridge for the rear wheel.

▼ Mudflaps can be made from a variety of materials, including the heavy duty membrane as used by builders to waterproof walls. Fit the plastic and then carefully trim to shape with scissors.

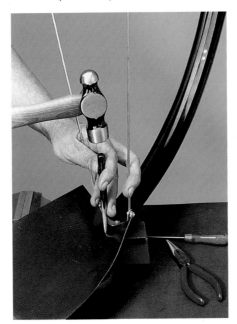

▼ Fender position is adjusted by loosening the clamp nuts on the fender stay brackets. Do not remove them, and make sure they are firmly tightened afterwards so that they don't come loose.

LIGHTING SYSTEMS

Function

A good lighting system gives you the confidence to bicycle after dark; its purpose is not only to enable you to see, but to make sure that you are seen by other road users. As bicycles are rarely fitted with lighting equipment when new, you will need to fit your own. There are basically two systems to choose from: battery powered ones (including rechargeable battery systems), and those that are generator-powered.

Battery systems require virtually no maintenance, but they are expensive to run unless you invest in sets of rechargeable batteries.

Generator systems are fitted permanently to the bicycle, and the power is generated by a tire-driven gener-

ator. They cost little to run, but all the lights go out when the rider stops moving. For safety reasons, it is essential to have a back-up for when this happens; battery powered takeover systems, which come into operation when the generator lights go out, are available.

There are two types of tire-driven generator. One, which is mounted beside the wheel, is set in motion when pressed against the sidewall. The other is usually mounted under the chainstays directly behind the bottom bracket, and is pressed against the tread of the tire. The former is very reliable, but the latter is liable to suffer from slippage in wet weather conditions.

For some reason, a tradition has

1 Clip one cord to the wire that goes into the generator. Clip the other cord to a metal part of the light bracket. If the bulb fails to light, the connection between the bracket and bulb is poor.

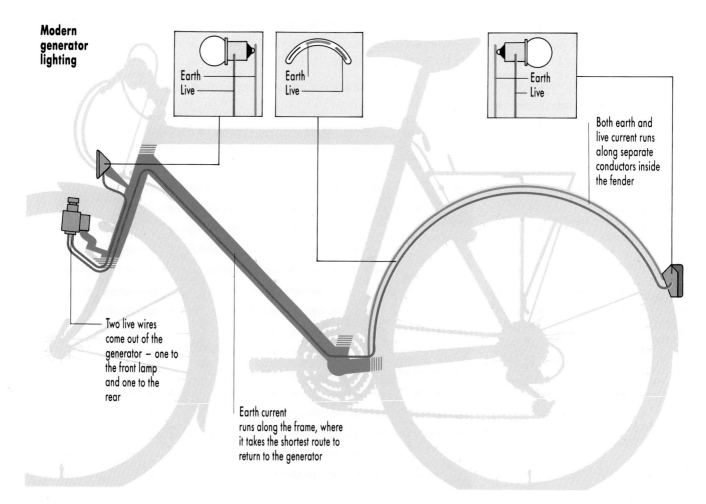

Modern generator lighting

Earth
Live

Earth
Live

Earth
Live

Both earth and live current runs along separate conductors inside the fender

Two live wires come out of the generator – one to the front lamp and one to the rear

Earth current runs along the frame, where it takes the shortest route to return to the generator

2 Now proceed to locate and check each connection along the circuit with one clip, while keeping the other clip on the end of the generator cord. Jiggle the clip to ensure that there is a good connection.

3 Continue to clip the cord to each connection. When the bulb fails to light up, you will know where the bad connection is. This will usually be where two parts are joined with a nut and bolt.

4 The connection can often be made good simply by undoing the nut and tightening it again, but you may have to dismantle the joint and clean the contacting surfaces with a file or emery cloth.

become established whereby the bicycle itself is used as the negative (or earth) return part of the generator system's electric circuit. The result is that there are a number of points where a poor connection can lead to failure of the whole system. This can be overcome by fitting a twin-wire system, but this has to be a do-it-yourself operation, because no such system is commercially available.

Frequent or early bulb failure is

usually caused by surges in current due to occasional high-speed riding – down a steep hill or ramp, for example. This is a greater problem if halogen bulbs are fitted, because halogen bulbs have a limited tolerance to current surges. Some modern systems are equipped with an integral voltage regulator. However, such a regulator can easily be fitted into the circuit of your system if it does not already have one.

Fault-finding
If one or other, or both, lights fail to work when the wheel is spun around when the generator is engaged, there are a number of checks you can carry out to trace the fault. You will need a 6-volt power source (a dry battery will do) and two long cords, each with a crocodile clip at the end.

First check each bulb by clipping the cords directly to the bulb's terminals. If they both fail to light, carry out the same check on another bulb, to make sure the battery and cords are good. Follow the method shown in the step-by-step photo sequence.

If your system is fitted with a halogen bulb, it is important that you do not handle the glass part of the bulb – use a piece of tissue paper.

▼ The sidewall generator is mounted beside the tire and is driven by being pressed against the sidewall. This is the more reliable drive system.

▼ The bottom bracket generator is usually mounted under the chainstays directly behind the bottom bracket, and is pressed against the tread of the tire.

Overhaul
The main purpose of the overhaul is to clean all the connections in the circuit, and to make sure that each connection will conduct the electric current efficiently. Over time, tiny amounts of water will seep between the metal contacts and cause a microscopically thin film of oxidation to form. The latter acts as an electrical insulator and should be cleaned away from time to time.

FURTHER INFORMATION

In this book, I have provided you with all the basic information you need simply to look after your bicycle. However, there will probably be differences between the bicycles I have used for illustrative purposes, and your own bicycle. If this is the case, you may well require some more information.

Manufacturers sometimes supply information with their new bicycles, but this rarely goes into any great detail. Furthermore, if you buy a second hand bicycle, you will be unlikely to receive any information with it.

It is also very likely that the manufacturer of your bicycle will only have designed the frame and forks, and then specified which components to use with them. So if you need further information, you should first identify the manufacturer of those other components of your bicycle, particularly the transmission. It may well be that the brakes are made by the same manufacturer.

Bicycle stores
If your local bicycle store is a good one, they may help you to identify the components fitted to your bicycle. But do not take unfair advantage of the help they may be prepared to give you. Remember that if you maintain your own bicycle, you will be doing them out of business to a certain extent – so make sure you at least buy all your spare parts and upgrades there. If you need help from the store, make sure you go in at a time when they are not busy, especially if you intend only to ask for help, and not to buy anything. Over a period of time, and provided you respect the fact that the bicycle store must sell bicycles and components to remain in business, you will find the help you receive to be of great value.

Books
If you want to increase your knowledge of how to carry out repairs and adjustments, you should consider buying a book for professional bicy-cle mechanics. Alternatively, look for books on bicycle technology.

Magazines
A wide choice of bicycling magazines is available today, and they are often an excellent source of advice and information. They frequently have workshop advice features, and information on new products that may be of interest to you. In addition, such magazines often feature articles on the very latest developments in bicycle technology.

Maintenance courses
The best way to learn bicycle maintenance skills is to attend a course. Seek a recommendation from your local bicycle store or attend a course run by a known name. Allow at least 25 hours of tuition if you want to learn enough to make the effort worthwhile. A few full-time short courses are offered for professional bicycle mechanics. As yet, however, there is no recognized bicycle maintenance qualification, nor is the quality of the instructors regulated.

Buying tools from stores
First acquire as many tool catalogs as possible, to find out what different manufacturers offer. Those described in this book have proved their worth time and time again, yet new tools are constantly being designed, produced and marketed.

Few bicycle stores stock anything like a comprehensive range of tools. The chances are that the store will have to order the tool for you, and then you will have to wait two or more weeks for delivery.

Buying tools by mail order
Buying specialist bicycle tools by mail order makes good sense, provided you select items that you know will be of a high quality. There is usually a much wider range of tools available for you to choose from in catalogs, and you should receive delivery within a few days or so.

The following manufacturers can supply technical information about their components. They will also supply specialist tools for maintaining and adjusting their own systems. Please try and provide them with as much information as possible about the components you have.

Dia Compe
PO Box 798
Fletcher
NC 28732

Grip Shift
SRAM Corporation
2039 West Carroll Avenue
Chicago
IL 60612

Fichtel & Sachs
22445 E La Palma Avenue
Suite J
Yorba Linda
CA 92686

Shimano
One Shimano Drive
PO Box 19615
Irvine
CA 92713

Sturmey Archer
1014 Carolina Drive
West Chicago
IL 60185

Sakae SunTour
18650 72nd Avenue South
Kent
WA 98032

Weinmann
3 Union Drive
Olney
IL 62450

As interest in bicycling increases, several manufacturers have produced a range of specialist bicycle maintenance tools. The following suppliers can send you a catalog and details of how to purchase, whether from your local bicycle store or direct, by mail order.

Park Tools
    3535 International Drive
    St Paul
    MN 55110

Var Tools
    Quality Bicycle Products
    7721 Pillsbury Avenue S.
    Richfield
    MN 55423

Cool Tool
    13524 Autumn Lane
    Chico
    CA 95926

Tacx Tools
    Cyclo Sport
    1540 Barklay Boulevard
    Buffalo Grove
    IL 60089

Eldi Tools
    KHS Bicycle Parts
    2 Union Drive
    Olney
    IL 62450

The Third Hand
(One-stop mail order depot)
    PO Box 212
    Mt Shasta
    CA 96067

A very few of the products mentioned in this book may be difficult to find in the stores or catalogs. If you experience any such difficulty, write to the addresses below where you can either purchase direct (by mail order), or find out where your nearest dealer is located.

Kestrel Workmate
    Kestrel Engineering
    Unit 10 Dartmouth Buildings
    Fort Fareham
    Hampshire
    PO14 1AH, UK

Rechargeable aerosol
    Finish Line Technologies
    23 Beach Street
    Islip
    NY 11751

Voltage regulator for 6V generator
    Reflectalite
    24 Orchard Road
    Brentford
    TW8 0QX, UK

Headmounted flashlight
    R F Design
    Seedbed Centre
    Davidson Way
    Romford
    RM7 0AZ, UK

There are many manufacturers of good-quality general tools. However, although a good selection is readily available in hardware stores, catalogs are always worth having for the extra information they provide. The following is a selection of suppliers who can provide you with a catalog.

Harbor Freight Tools
    3491 Mission Oaks Blvd
    Camarillo
    CA930116010

Stanley Tools
    600 Myrtle Street
    New Britain
    CT 06050

Sears Stores
    Most major towns and cities have a Sears Store which carries a wide choice of 'Craftsman' tools

The Author gratefully acknowledges the help and assistance of the following:

- Dave Banks of Bickers Anglia
- Barbara Berkowitz
- Frank Berto
- Jane Brannan
- Angela Brookes of Neill Tools
- Kim Cave of Stanley Tools
- Judy and Bill Cowie
- Sue Darlow
- Simon Ellison of Ron Kitching
- Jim Elson of FiveStar Products
- Stuart Falshaw of RFDesign
- Nick Fish of Trek UK
- Kim Forsyth
- Peter Holden of Everything Cycling
- Graeme Gibson for Fishers of Finchley
- Karen Kenelly of Madison Cycles
- Debbie Korzenek of Raaco Storage Systems
- Peter Mearbeck of Record Tools
- Fred Milson
- Christine Patient
- Jason Smith
- Alan Walker of Kestrel Engineering
- Mark Welch of Black & Decker
- Nancy Woodhead of Coldstream Cycles

Bicycle maintenance courses:

Barnett Bicycle Institute
    2755 Ore Mill Drive
    Colorado Springs
    CO 80904

United Bicycle Institute
    PO Box 128
    Ashland
    OR 97520 - 0128

INDEX